A man who seeks revenge digs two graves.

–*Chinese proverb*

THE SECOND GRAVE

•

A Case for the Abolition of the Death Penalty

Carl Wedekind

Published by
THE KENTUCKY COALITION TO
ABOLISH THE DEATH PENALTY

This book is dedicated to those
who have suffered from violence.

ACKNOWLEDGMENTS

There are many who helped in the writing of this book, and I am indebted to them for their scholarship, their insights, and blessedly, their encouragement.

First, my love and my thanks to Stephanie Wedekind, my editor *in familia*, whose clarity in editing and patience in everything, made possible the accomplishment of this work. To our children, Moira Wedekind, Araby Thornewill, and her husband, Judah, and Annie Wedekind, for their interest, insights, and encouragement, I am both pleased and grateful.

Dr. James C. Klotter, professor of history at Georgetown College and the State Historian of Kentucky, reviewed at my request chapters one and two of this book covering the history of violence in Kentucky and the history of the death penalty statutes, and his corrections and suggestions were invaluable. I thank him for his generosity in sharing with a stranger his time and his broad knowledge of the subject matter.

Dr. Gary Potter, Professor of Police Studies at Eastern Kentucky University, likewise gave freely of his skills in critiquing the manuscript. His suggestions were on mark, and his encouraging words to this author were needed and appreciated.

Steve Bright, Director of the Southern Center for Human Rights in Atlanta (and a native Kentuckian), probably knows more about the inequities of the death penalty and does more to combat them than any other individual in America. He gave generously of his time and knowledge in making suggestions and criticizing this work, and I thank him for his valuable help and his friendship.

There is a group of individuals from different professions and backgrounds, who have for many years been the heart and soul of the death penalty abolition movement in Kentucky, whom I asked to review and critique this work while it was in progress. They are: Rowly Brucken, Fr. Patrick Delahanty, George Edwards, Maria Hines, Everett Hoffman, Mary Lou Houck, Arch Taylor Jr., and Scott Wegenast. Each one took the time to do this, and their comments, criticisms, and suggestions were critical in shaping the final work. I am privileged to know these individuals, and I thank each one of them for their interest and their help.

I am indebted to Ed Monahan, Randy Wheeler, and Rebecca Ballard DiLoreto of the Kentucky Department of Public Advocacy for their assistance in gathering data, for their suggestions, and for the use of the library and archives at the DPA office in Frankfort.

I thank James Fenwick, law student at the Brandeis School of Law, University of Louisville, for his able pro bono help in legal research at the beginning of this project and to Kaye Gallagher for her editing assistance at the end.

I am also obliged to the archivists at the Statistical Unit of the Kentucky State Police, the Kentucky Department for Libraries and Archives, the Louisville Free Public Library Kentucky Section and at the Filson Club for their assistance and courtesies.

With all this said, it is obvious that the merits of this book can be shared by many; the mistakes are undeniably mine.

CW

INTRODUCTION

Civilization cannot be preserved by conduct which is in itself barbaric.

Victor Gollancz

The passion for the gathering of these materials and the writing of this book comes from my realization that the imposition of the death penalty solves nothing, and, in fact, adds to the problem of violence in Kentucky.

The journey I have taken has been a search into the history of violence and of the death penalty in Kentucky, to see what can be learned, and to determine where we should go from here. My research uncovered exciting, often fearsome tales, many of which we can be glad are in the past.

I find that these histories point unerringly to an evolution in our conduct; a continuing, restless struggle to make life in Kentucky less burdened by senseless violence, free of the bloody past, and open to achieving a safer, more sane society.

Following the histories, I turn to the arguments put forth in the death penalty debate as it currently flows, and I search for the truth in each proposition, as borne out by our history, by our personal experience, and by our judgment.

The facts, statistics, and anecdotes gathered here show, in my judgment, that the death penalty serves no purpose other than the prolonging of our bloody history. There is no cogent reason, there is no individual or social benefit derived from the state's exercising of the death penalty.

Substantial portions of our wealth and our energies are now devoted to the issues and the conduct of executions. I believe this wealth and these energies can be spent more wisely in responding to the needs of our children, and the causes of capital crime.

It is time that we end executions, and discover that we will have a less violent community without the second grave.

CONTENTS

CHAPTER I
A BRIEF HISTORY OF VIOLENCE IN KENTUCKY

*"I have never seen a Kentuckian without a gun, a pack
of cards, and a bottle of whiskey in my life."*
General Andrew Jackson

The death penalty in Kentucky is not an isolated policy of violence standing alone, but is very much a part of our state's history of violence. We need to look at that history to understand why we have the death penalty, and why we will abolish it.

The history is long and colorful, to be sure, but we find no heavy hand of constancy in our violence. We do observe, from the very beginning, sharp struggles between forces for peaceful resolution and the forces of violence, and increasingly the forces for peaceful resolution are dominant.

We began our state's history with laws of enlightenment condemning the death penalty, and then followed a course proving that Kentucky's "dark and bloody ground" legend was no myth. But each time we headed for the depths, we stopped, regrouped, and found a better way.

We know the stories of Daniel Boone, the Indian raids, the assassination of Governor Goebel, and the Hatfields and the McCoys. They are all familiar tales. But not often do we hear about the Know Nothings and Bloody Monday, the bushwhackers, the lynch mobs, guerrilla raids, the Black Patch War, union busting, and race riots. We will begin by looking into that history.

BEGINNINGS

The story of violence in Kentucky begins in 1742, and contrary to conventional wisdom, that violence did not begin with the Indians. A group of Virginians, led by John Peter Salling, John Howard and his son, Josiah, were exploring the "western waters"and reached the Ohio River. Unfortunately, they met a party of Frenchmen who attacked them and captured Peter Salling. The French claimed this territory and hauled Salling off to New Orleans to explain his trespass to the authorities.[1]

In time the explorers became settlers, and Indian as well as French resistance grew.

It is difficult now to imagine Kentucky in the 18th century. Whether you came by boat down the Ohio or walked over the mountains and through the Cumberland Gap, once into Kentucky you were surrounded by forest, a pervasive darkness from the canopy. Simple survival was difficult.[2] There was the danger from Indians and bears and accidents, and the constant need to gather food and have shelter. Each person old enough had a gun and shot and powder. Life depended on it.

There were no permanent Indian villages in Kentucky when the explorers arrived. The settlements of the Iroquois, Wyandottes, and Shawnees were to the north and those of the Cherokee, Creek, Catawha and Chickasaw to the south. The Indian interests in Kentucky were hunting rights.

1. Thomas D. Clark, A *History of Kentucky* (The Jesse Stuart Foundation, 1988) page 20, hereinafter cited as Clark. A letter from Dr. Clark, dated March 18, 1998, states, "So far as I know the Peter Salling incident was the first act of violence in Kentucky. I say this with reservation because the record might be foggy for the earliest movements, and on this subject."
2. Harriette Simpson Arnow in the wonderful *Seedtime on the Cumberland* (The University Press of Kentucky, 1983) describes the hardship of frontier life and recounts the remarkable skills necessary for living in and using the woods that were mastered by the surviving settlers. See pages 139 to 144.

In the Treaty of Paris in 1763 the French ceded claims to the Kentucky territory to the British and shortly thereafter George III issued a Proclamation declaring the land west of the Appalachians reserved for the Indians and the English fur traders.[3] The push west came to a halt, and because of the hardships, the Indian raids, and the inability of the Virginia colony to provide protection, many settlers returned east across the mountains and a period of peace ensued until the American Revolution in 1776. Then the struggle for the land in Kentucky began anew among the Americans, the British, the French and the Indians. As the Americans defeated each of these foes the push for settlement into Kentucky grew mightily. The goal was land, and the wealth the land could produce.[4]

There was serious violence on the Kentucky frontier between the settlers and the Indians from the very beginning until well into the 19th century. The Indians raided the white settlements in Kentucky, and the whites raided the Indian settlements north of the Ohio. There were many deaths, but this struggle with the indigenous Indians is beyond the scope of this review. Here I will be limited to the evolution of violence among the cultures from Europe and Africa.

From the earliest days there were conflicting land claims in Kentucky. These included claims from the English Crown, the Transylvania Company on land acquired by its treaty with the Cherokee at Sycamore Shoales, claims for service in the French and Indian War, and from the new United States government and State of Virginia for Revolutionary War service, and, not to be forgotten, claims from settlers who had come to Kentucky, built a cabin, planted crops, and survived.

Virginia passed land laws and established land courts, but there was no solution to the many overlapping claims for

3. Thomas D. Clark, *A History of Kentucky* (The Jesse Stuart Foundation, 1988) page 27.
4. Ibid. page 63.

land, which totaled thousands of acres more land than there was in Kentucky. Nor was there a solution to the surveying errors committed by amateur surveyors, which made the establishment of the best of claims wildly uncertain. The setting became a bonanza for eastern lawyers drawn by the conflicts and a disaster for those claimants with the least survival skills, many of whom, like Daniel Boone, lost and left. Through it all there developed a broad and deep distrust of the law, the government, and outsiders. Some of these land disputes, and the feuds they engendered, exist to this very day.[5]

After ten conventions, Kentucky separated from Virginia and became a state in 1792, although there was a strong sentiment among many settlers to go it alone and become a separate power.[6]

One of the early acts of the new state was the Kentucky Resolutions of 1798 making it very clear to the Congress of the United States that Kentucky had and reserved the right to decide on its own which acts of Congress were constitutional and which were not.[7]

The independence of the state and of its citizens was manifest. Personal disputes, particularly those of honor, were settled personally. There was little tradition of settling disputes in court, and for those on the Kentucky frontier, the courts were distant and ineffective. The custom and the practice was fighting, and the methods could be boxing, wrestling, eye gouging, ear biting, or whatever was necessary to win.[8]

5. George III's 1763 Proclamation forbidding settlement of Kentucky territory made any Virginia land laws for the territory questionable. After the Declaration of Independence in 1776 Virginia could and did pass laws to regulate land warrants and the adjudication of claims. But there was no survey system nor qualifications to be a surveyor. Surveyor Daniel Boone's son said his father surveyed well so long as it was a rectangle. In 1779, Land Courts were established in Kentucky which attracted lawyers such as John Breckinridge and Henry Clay, and hundreds of land warrants were issued. If a land claimant lost, his only appeal was across the mountains to Richmond, at a cost of time and money rarely available.
6. Clark, page 84.
7. Ibid. page 109.
8. Ibid. page 67-68.

Since each man had a gun, the choices were broadened. If you were of a mind, you could challenge an offender to a duel, or simply wait your opportunity and bring him to justice with an unannounced shot from a hiding place.[9]

These killings most often were in isolated communities and each event was brooded on until there was revenge upon revenge, and more family feuds were born and nurtured through the generations. [10]

When Kentuckians weren't fighting in their own "hollars" or meadows, they were off fighting elsewhere. Many of the settlers had fought in the Revolutionary War and come to Kentucky to collect their land grant, and they and many others were quick to go and fight elsewhere when the opportunity arose.

The War of 1812 was one of those opportunities. Kentucky troops were led by no less than Governor Isaac Shelby and Congressman Richard M. Johnson. Kentuckians played a major role in the land battles in the northwest against the English and the Indians. Colonel Johnson led his Kentucky troops across the Detroit River forcing the English Regulars under Colonel Henry Proctor and a large band of Indians led by Tecumseh to retreat after burning Detroit. The forces clashed

9. Ibid. page 73.
10. In 1967, following the assassination of Martin Luther King and Bobby Kennedy, President Lyndon Johnson appointed a National Commission on the Causes and Prevention of Violence, and named Dr. Milton S. Eisenhower as Chair. The Commission Report is a series of studies on the subject by scholars, and particularly pertinent here is Chapter 4 of the Report, "The Frontier Tradition: An Invitation to Violence" by Professor Joe B. Franz, of the University of Texas History Department. See: *The History of Violence in America* (Bantam Books, New York, 1969).

Editors Ted Robert Gurr and Hugh Davis Graham state on page 1 of the Introduction: "Almost every major act of violence in our history, whether public or private, has antagonized one group at the same time that it satisfied another... The grievances and satisfactions of violence have so reinforced one another that we have become a rather bloody minded people in both action and reaction. We are likely to remain so as long as so many of us think that violence is an ultimate solution to social problems."
Also see Clark, page 414.

on the upper Thames River, and it is said that Colonel Johnson in the heat of the battle shot and killed Tecumseh in a face-off, and the remaining Indian warriors took flight.[11]

Kentuckians also volunteered and fought in the southwest division in the battle of New Orleans, where General Andrew Jackson was in command. When an aide reported that the recently arrived Kentucky troops had not been supplied with rifles, and complained of being unarmed, Jackson said, "I don't believe it. I have never seen a Kentuckian without a gun and a pack of cards and a bottle of whiskey in my life."[12]

As the wars were won and the Kentucky frontier became less hazardous the population increase was remarkable. Before the revolution, Kentucky's population was noted at 150; by the time of statehood in 1792 there were 63,000 whites and 12,000 slaves. By 1800, eight years later, whites had almost tripled to 180,000, and slaves more than tripled to 41,000.[13]

Slaves had a considerable value by doing the difficult clearing of land in the settlement days, and their numbers continued to increase, with imports peaking in the 1830s. As the clearing was completed and the larger farms were broken into smaller tracts, slaves were less economically beneficial, and Kentucky moved from being a consumer of slaves to a major trader. Trading companies were located in Lexington and Louisville, buying unneeded or troublesome slaves from Kentucky owners, holding them in private jails, and shipping them by boat to Natchez and New Orleans to respond profitably to the continuing demand of the deep south for slave labor. It was a brutal business. [14]

The financial panic of 1819 and the depression that

11. Clark, page 131-132.
12. Ibid. page 133.
13. Lowell H. Harrison and James C. Klotter, A New History of Kentucky (University Press of Kentucky, Lexington, Ky., 1997) page 98, hereinafter cited as Harrison and Klotter. Also see: Clark, page 193.
14. Harrison and Klotter, page 168.

followed brought enormous problems to the people of Kentucky as well as the rest of the nation.

The struggle was between borrowers and lenders. The borrowers were broke and could do no other than default on their notes, and when the lenders foreclosed, the borrowers turned to their legislators for help. Help was forthcoming in Debt Relief Acts which, when tested, were held unconstitutional by Kentucky courts. The situation was so critical and the pressures so great, that the legislature voted to disband the court, and established a new court more disposed to its wishes. Politics became very heavy between the "New Court" and "Old Court" factions, and custody of records was settled by guns in an assault on the Old Court records room and the forcible removal of everything in sight. Historians now marvel that civil war did not break out in Kentucky, but to the state's credit the struggle remained primarily a political one, and as economic conditions improved, the pressures eased and ultimately the Old Court and constitutional government won out.[15]

One characteristic of a frontier society and its clashes of ideas and cultures is vigilantism. [16] In early Kentucky vigilantism arose where there was no established law and order, and the understood common law of the community was enforced by those offended, against the offender. There were no jails or system of fines. The only alternative to sufferance was violence.

The earliest record in Kentucky of "Regulators" as organized mobs, was in Russellville in 1793 and on the Green and Little Barren Rivers in the 1790s. While vigilante justice was widespread in the early 1800s, the records reflect that much of the heaviest action was in Western Kentucky. Regulators were active in Christian, Todd, and Hopkins counties in the 1820s and in 1845, in Muhlenberg County from 1825 to 1850,

15. Ibid. page 109, et seq.; Clark, page 147.
16. Ted Robert Gurr and Hugh Davis Graham, editors, *The History of Violence in America* (Bantam Books, New York, 1969) page 105.

and in Paducah in the 1840s.[17]

The Regulators were devoted to punishing horse thieves and "bad men," with occasional sorties against the poor and the lazy. Due process was the leader's decision to act, and the punishment was swift and most often brutal. The process provided a quick and, to the Regulators, satisfactory answer to a community problem.

DUELING

Kentucky's landed gentry of the 19th century readily accepted the concept of a "gentleman's honor," and were quick to fight a duel to defend their honor. The *code duelo* was set forth in a 33-page pamphlet, published by the Honorable John Lyde Wilson of Charleston, South Carolina, and the rules were followed to the letter.

Historians count at least 41 formal duels that received notoriety in Kentucky; they calculate there were many more that escaped detection. [18]

The first recorded formal duel took place before statehood, in 1790 near Danville, between Captain James Strong and Henry Craig. The latter was the better shot, and defended his honor by killing the Captain. [19]

Most duels were fought with pistols at ten paces, or 30 feet. If rifles or shotguns were the weapon of choice, the defenders of honor were required to stand further apart.

There were enough duels early on that the state legislature in 1799 passed an act prohibiting dueling (and gambling), and levied a fine of $150 to $500 upon conviction. Subsequent legislation added a prison term. But the frontiersmen

17. Ibid. page 222.
18. Samuel M. Wilson, *History of Kentucky, Vol. II*, (S.J. Clarke Publishing Co., Chicago, 1928), pages 282, 283.
19. The expert on Kentucky duels is J. Winston Coleman Jr., and the accounts presented here are taken from his book, *Famous Kentucky Duels* (Henry Clay Press, Lexington, 1969).

enjoyed the spectacle of dueling by the "gentlemen," and the law was rarely enforced.

Many well-known Kentuckians engaged in dueling, including John Rowan, the leading attorney of Bardstown, and later a United States senator. He and Dr. James Chambers got to drinking and gambling one night until in the wee hours the whiskey talk turned to the classics, and a royal argument ensued as to who, the lawyer or the doctor, was the greater scholar of the dead languages. Although the two gentlemen could barely stand, they did manage to throw a few blows before being taken home, with the argument undecided.

Upon sobering up, they remembered enough to know their honors had been sullied, and the duel that followed determined that, best or not, Dr. Chambers was the dead scholar. Other well-known Kentuckians who participated in duels were General Thomas Kennedy, Henry Clay, and Humphrey Marshall. Even Andrew Jackson found time to duel while visiting in Kentucky.

In the Constitutional Convention creating Kentucky's third constitution of 1850 the framers turned against the code duelo, and Article VIII, Sec. 20 provided that anyone engaging in a duel or serving as a second, "shall be deprived of the right to hold any office of honor or profit in this Commonwealth, and shall be punished otherwise in such manner as the General assembly may prescribe by law." [20]

The combination of the prohibitions of the new Constitution and the experiences of the Civil War brought an end to dueling in Kentucky, and the last duel recorded was in 1867 between Littleton Wells, 22, and Saford Roberts, 24, who both loved the same Kentucky belle. When she chose Roberts, Wells

20. In fulfillment of this provision, anyone taking an Oath of Office in Kentucky, or becoming a lawyer, must swear: "that since the adoption of the present (third) Constitution, I, being a citizen of this state, have not fought a duel with deadly weapons within this state nor out of it; nor have I sent or accepted a challenge to fight a duel with deadly weapons; nor have I acted as second in carrying a challenge, or aided or assisted any person thus offending."

was offended, and challenged Roberts to a duel. The lady ended up with neither gentlemen — Roberts received a bullet to his heart, while simultaneously, Wells received the same to his head.

And the chapter was over.

IMMIGRANTS

In the six decades from 1800 to the Civil War, Kentucky's population increased from 180,000 to more than 900,000, and the slave population grew from 40,000 to 225,000. The freed blacks were less then one percent of the total. Interestingly, in 1850 the white population was over 90 percent from the British Isles: English (57 percent), Scotch-Irish and Scotch (18 percent), Welsh (9 percent), and Irish (8 percent). [21]

The revolution in Germany in 1848, and the Irish potato famine vastly increased the flow of immigrants to the new country and its frontier. Many of the Irish and Germans coming to Kentucky settled in Louisville, and though they remained a very small percentage of the overall population, they became a decided presence in Louisville, and at this time we see the onset of nativism.[22]

American nativism started with the Revolutionary War, and played a dominant role in a brief stormy period of Kentucky history shortly before the outbreak of the Civil War.

As the slavery issue became more and more focused, the Whig Party disintegrated with internal dissension over that issue and a new party, the American Party, grew to fill the void and to take on the Democrats. The essence of the new message was "America for the Americans," and this message sounded wise to many Kentuckians who feared the solid immigrant opposition to slavery, and the menace of an increas-

21. Harrison and Klotter, page 100.
22. Ibid. page 122.

ing Catholic population owing obeisance to the Pope in Rome. The American Party, known as the "Know Nothings" because of their secretiveness, won local elections in Lexington, Covington, and Louisville. In the general elections of August 6, 1855, they swept the state, electing the governor and a majority of the state legislators. Their methods at the polls in Louisville led to the most fearful riot that the city or the state has ever seen.

"The general issue," according to George D. Prentice, editor of the widely read Louisville Journal, "is between Americanism and foreignism."[23] Editor Prentice opined on the Catholics: "The Romish Corporation, under the pretense of being the bride of Christ, has ever been the prostitute of Satan." He urged voters shortly before the August 6 election to defeat the "overwheening and most pestilent influence of the foreign swarms."[24]

This the Know Nothings did, by sending their own enforcers to the polls early election morning and not allowing anyone to vote who did not display the yellow ticket of the American Party.[25] Their actions resulted in long lines and fist fights at the polling places of the Irish and German wards.

In the afternoon the enforcers were joined by other rowdies in roving bands committing mayhem on any foreigner they could find, ransacking Catholic churches and foreign-owned buildings, and finally climaxing that night by their burning an entire block of Irish homes. The fire department was kept from extinguishing the fires, and as residents attempted to escape the flames, they were shot.

23. Ibid. page 123.
24. From a paper by Thomas P. Baldwin entitled "Bloody Monday Memorial Services" in the archives of the Kentuckiana Germanic Heritage Society, kept in the old rectory of Saint John's Evangelical Church, Clay and Market streets, Louisville. There were three German language newspapers in Louisville at the time, and copies of one of them, the Louisville Anzeiger, are available in the Society's archives, which detail many aspects of the riot of August 6, 1855, in Louisville.
25. Baldwin, page 2.

Historians generally report 20 or 22 killed, but the truth is no one knows because the authorities responsible for the records were Know Nothings. Independent sources have estimated the killing at over 100. However large the number, the day is forever known as "Bloody Monday."[26]

THE CIVIL WAR ERA

The Civil War brought into focus some sharp dichotomies in the mores of the Kentucky populace. The overwhelming sentiment opposed secession, and by far the greater number went to fight for the Union.[27] Yet, when the war was over, Kentucky had difficulty freeing its own slaves, and state politics were taken over wholesale by the returning Rebel Democrats, shutting out the Union Democrats, the new Republicans and the returning Union veterans. The 13th, 14th, and 15th Amendments to the United States Constitution were never ratified by the Kentucky Legislature until civil rights leaders forced the issue, 100 years later, in the 1970s.

A new and different violence surfaced during the Civil War and its aftermath. To the native-born violence of the early frontier was added a nastier, meaner violence of hate and fear, bred of ignorance and loss, and uncaring. It seemed that the Know Nothing riots were an omen of what was to come.

The violence began early. Volunteers for the South would move in groups cautiously through the gaps of the eastern Kentucky mountains to join the Confederate Army, and many would be picked off by sharp shooting "patriots" hiding in the bush, acting on their own volition, and earning the title of "Bushwackers." [28]

The armies of both the North and the South repeat-

26. Baldwin, page 2.
27. Clark, page 336. Dr. Clark reports between 30,000 and 40,000 Kentuckians enlisted in the Confederate service and approximately 64,000 fought in the Union ranks.
28. Ibid. page 321.

edly invaded Kentucky during the war, and large numbers of stragglers and deserters were left in their wake. Sometimes they would group together to become guerrilla bands; small groups of men, lawless desperadoes, plundering, burning, robbing, and raping defenseless individuals and families in their scattered communities. As the war progressed the guerrillas came increasingly from the Rebel army, roaming over almost every section of the state. [29]

The brutality of the guerrilla raids became so horrendous Union commanders in Kentucky ordered the arrest of five prominent Rebel sympathizers held hostage for every citizen killed by guerrillas. [30]

In 1864, Union General Stephen Burbridge ordered four guerrillas killed for every Unionist murdered, and many innocent Confederate prisoners were brought out to meet the quota. In just one incident, two Confederate soldiers were publicly hanged in Lexington and six in Green County to avenge the death of two Union soldiers.

The leaders of many of the bands were known by name: Quantrill, Hall, James, Long, and Pence were a few. The retaliation of the Yankee forces became so virulent and oppressive that Governor Bramlette broke off his friendly relations with President Lincoln and ordered an enlistment of ten thousand volunteers to help put down the guerrilla warfare.[31]

This random, mindless violence on all sides was part of Kentucky life, not only during the war but for a number of years thereafter. Lincoln's Emancipation Proclamation did not apply to Kentucky slaves because the state had not seceded from the Union, and slave holders demanded compensation if their slaves were to be freed. Congress never acceded to these demands. During the war slaves were not freed by their Ken-

---

29. Hambleton Tapp and James C. Klotter, *Kentucky: Decades of Discord 1865-1900*, (The Kentucky Historical Society, Frankfort, Ky. 1977) page 2.
30. Clark, page 333.
31. Ibid. page 334.

tucky masters, but one way to freedom was to escape and enlist in the Union Army.

The idea of Negro slaves fighting as soldiers under a Kentucky flag was way beyond the reckoning of Kentucky's white males on either side of the struggle. Fighting was for white men, fighting for their honor and the honor of their state. Kentuckians always overfilled their volunteer quota for any and every war and, in the case of the Civil War, on both sides. These emotions were so deep, the feelings so bitter that the War Department ceased accepting black enlistees in Kentucky. They later recommenced black enlistment, but herded all the enlistees, including their women and children, into camps near Louisville where their numbers rose to 28,000 by 1865. Many were able to slip out of camp and cross the river to ease their troubles and leave the fury of their former owners on the other side. [32]

In 1862, the U.S. government appointed General Jeremiah T. Boyle Commander of the "Department of Kentucky." He was a driven man. He demanded Union loyalty, and he ordered the arrest and detention of any citizen reported to bear Southern leanings. He required official oaths of loyalty for public officials and for lawyers, preachers, doctors, and teachers alike. [33] Arrests on trumped up charges and mistreatment of civilians by Union forces became so rampant that a Resolution was introduced in the United States Senate calling for an investigation of conditions in Kentucky.

The state elections of 1863 were a contest between the Union Democrat Bramlette for Governor and the Regular Democrat Wickliffe. It was important to the Union forces that the Union Democrats win, and they did by a wide margin because the Union Army either jailed or exiled or thoroughly intimidated the leaders of the opposition. The high-handed tactics of the Union Officers produced such rancor that in the

32. Ibid. page 334-5.
33. Ibid. page 345.

national election of 1864, despite Union interference, Lincoln lost the presidential election to McClellan in Kentucky by a margin of over two to one. [34]

In the countryside the widespread guerrilla bands were joined by a unique group known as the Partisan Rangers, authorized by the Confederate command to operate behind Union lines. Out of touch with authority, and with little military restraint, their members became marauders and were no better then the deserter- filled guerrilla bands. General Rosser wrote General Robert E. Lee that the Rangers were "a band of thieves, stealing, pillaging, plundering and doing every manner of mischief and crime."[35]

Not to be outdone, the Union-controlled legislature established a Union Home Guard, charged with the responsibility to suppress any and all pro-Confederate activities in the counties. The Home Guard was armed, with few restraints, and regulated their counties to their own whim and fancy. Gross acts of violence and injustices occurred, and another group was added to compete with the guerrillas.[36]

The Civil War increased the level of violence in Kentucky until violence was being experienced without even a pretense of reason. Men with guns and horses ran roughshod and ruled. The cultural upheaval at the end of slavery added a new layer of white hatred and intolerance to the existing lawlessness. From this crucible came the Ku Klux Klan, the Night Riders, and lynching.

Black slaves were subject to punishment by their owners, but as property they had great value, and were well protected by the law from harm by outside white violence. With the end of the war that protection vanished. The slaves were free and vulnerable.

34. Ibid. page 348.
35. Hamilton Tapp and James C. Klotter, *Kentucky: Decades of Discord 1865-1900* (The Kentucky Historical Society, 1977) page 6.
36. Ibid. page 6-7.

Blacks seeking a place to live, to work, and to start a new life were harassed and beaten, run off, and frequently murdered. State officials refused to respond to the black pleas for protection and refused or were unable to prevent outbreaks of violence. Everyday conditions for blacks deteriorated to such an extent that the federal government in 1866 extended the Freedmen's Bureau to Kentucky. The Freedmen's Bureau was an agency of the United States War Department charged with providing for the welfare of the newly liberated blacks of the south,[37] and Kentucky was the only non-seceding state to be so supervised. But this action accomplished little as white violence quickly expanded to include agents of the Freedmen's Bureau. [38]

Black Union soldiers returning home to free their wives and children were attacked by roving white bands. Groups of blacks petitioned Congress for protection from white mobs, citing instances of lynching and other attacks, but they got no relief. The Freedmen's Bureau agents were thoroughly intimidated.[39]

As a result of the violence against blacks, many moved from rural areas to Louisville and Lexington, or out of Kentucky entirely. Blacks made up more than 20 percent of Kentucky's population in 1860 and that dropped precipitously to 14 percent by 1900, and the percentage has continued to decrease to this day. [40]

With the emancipation of the slaves came the beginning of lynching, and this history extends in Kentucky for some 70 years, from Reconstruction to 1934.

Lynching is defined as the practice whereby mobs capture individuals suspected of a crime and execute them by hang-

37. For a detailed discussion of the Freedmen's Bureau, see Albert Castel, *The Presidency of Andrew Johnson* (The Regents Press of Kansas, Lawrence, 1979).
38. George C. Wright, *Racial Violence in Kentucky*, 1865-1940 (Louisiana State University Press, Baton Rouge, 1990) page 2.
39. Ibid. page 3.
40. Ibid. page 4.

ing, without any process of law. The key to this phenomenon is community approval, either explicit by general participation, or implicit, by the acquittal of the killers.

This description applies at least 353 times in Kentucky from March 1866, when a black man, Bertraud, was hanged in Paris on suspicion of rape, to September 1934, when a black man, Scott, was hanged in Hazard on suspicion of murder. [41] In each instance mob violence prevailed; sometimes cool and calculating, other times outrageously brutal, madly vicious. Kentuckians were a people angered by the results of a war most of them had supported. They were, by and large, poorly educated, economically depressed, and fearful of the new competition of black labor and black sexuality.

In 1866, there were nine mob lynchings, increasing to 21 in 1869, and reaching 36 in 1870 — three every month, in 18 different counties throughout the state. Twenty-seven victims were black, but the reasons for the white anger are largely lost. It was recorded however, that two black men, James Parker and William Tempin, were hanged in August 1870, for being Republicans, and a black woman, Mrs. John Sims, was hanged in September 1870 in Henry County because her husband was a Republican.[42]

Some mobs arose spontaneously, as on the rumor of a black man raping a white woman; others were organized more carefully to bring retribution for a real or imagined wrong to society, but increasingly the moving force behind much of the mob violence in Kentucky was the Ku Klux Klan.

The Klan took on the agents of the Freedmen's Bureau in a struggle over the opportunities, the status, and the education of blacks. For the most part the Klan held sway, and the vast majority of whites, including elected officials, refused to denounce the mobs or to pass anti-mob legislation.[43]

41. Ibid. page 307.
42. Ibid. page 310.
43. Ibid. pages 17, 25-26.

By 1868, blacks were holding meetings to organize their participation in the political process, and to achieve their voting rights under the 15th Amendment. The Klan harassed the ministers and educators who spoke at such meetings and commenced a general campaign to intimidate or run off any real or potential Republican voters. In politics, the Klan was color blind. In a four-month period in the eastern Kentucky counties of Magoffin, Perry, Breathitt, and Wolfe, the Klan murdered 19 men because they were Republicans, and they were all white.[44]

The Klan had so little fear of authority that 75 masked men marched to the jail in Frankfort and forcedly freed Thomas Scroggins, a white man charged with the brutal murder of a black man. Their stated reason: no white man should be forced to defend himself in court against the word of a black man.

The Klan was so powerful in 1872 that they and brother renegades controlled 15 counties in central Kentucky, usurping local governments, and becoming the law.[45]

Black Americans freed of slavery sought an education and the Freedmen's Bureau along with missionary societies conducted a major drive in 1867 to establish schools for blacks throughout Kentucky. No sooner did the schools open, the Klan blew them up. Allen County officials reported that a black school could not exist unless "protected by an armed force." In Louisville, white businessmen agreed to lease a building for a black school, and a mob burned it down.[46]

The lynching continued after the Reconstruction period and peaked in number, if not in brutality, during the decade 1890-1899. After the turn of the 20th century lynching continued but gradually decreased into the 1930s. Over these years, 75 percent of those murdered were black.[47]

44. Ibid. page 26.
45. Ibid. page 27.
46. Ibid. page 27.
47. Ibid. pages 307 to 323.

I will briefly describe one lynching. It is a brutal example, but no more so than many. An amazing aspect is the openness of the mob rituals.

Richard Coleman was a black man who lived and worked in Maysville. He was arrested and charged with the rape and murder of a white woman in October 1889. Before he could be tried, a mob gathered and took Coleman from the sheriff, who offered no resistance. Not content with just hanging, the mob set fire to Coleman; hundreds of people gathered to watch and feed the fire. When Coleman was dead, the mob dragged his body through the streets of Maysville, and it is said people cut off fingers and toes as souvenirs. No one wore masks. Everyone knew who was involved. No charges were brought.[48]

As the century wore on, the Klan, the Regulators and others remained as major problems erupting here and there. Though some politicians and some newspapers called for reform, the white public generally watched excitedly when it was a local event, and otherwise either ignored or accepted the lawless mobs as a part of Kentucky life.

KENTUCKY FEUDS

After the Freedmen's Bureau Agents left the state and Reconstruction was no longer the issue, increased attention was paid, particularly by the national press, to another fascinating form of Kentucky violence — family feuds. To qualify as a real feud in the Kentucky tradition, families or clans had to engage in hostilities over a long period of time, and the motives on both sides had to be vengeance.

Most of the feuds after the Civil War were in the mountains of Eastern Kentucky, but one of the earliest and most famous arose in the foothills, in Garrard County. The Hill-

48. Harrison and Klotter, page 251.

Evans feud dated back to an 1820 controversy, which erupted again in the 1850s, was renewed during the Civil War, and closed in 1877 when after a final skirmish the Hill-Evans feud reached the acme of feuds — only one male participant remained alive. History fails to record whether he was a Hill or an Evans.[49]

Family clan members sometime grew to be Regulators, taking on wider bands of controversy, and one such was the Underwood-Stamper, or Holbrook feud in Carter County. This fighting went on long after the Civil War and at various times the Underwood clan (in their home called Fort Underwood) withstood the attacks of not only the Stamper family, but the Regulators, and a force of state militia. This feud resulted in as many as 30 deaths.

The Martin-Tolliver-Logan feud began over a political argument and reached such intensity it became known as the Rowan County War, resulting in at least 20 murders and 16 wounded during a three-year period in the 1880s. The Tolliver faction, through a series of murders, gained control of the city of Morehead and its court system. The Logans appealed to the governor for help. When that request was refused, the Logans purchased quantities of rifles and ammunition, armed almost 200 men, and in June 1887, surrounded the city of Morehead, including the Tollivers. A wild shoot-out followed. Buildings were set on fire, and as the Tollivers tried to flee they were picked off one by one by the Logan forces. When the dust settled, the victorious Logans requested and received pardons from the governor.

In Harlan County, the Howard-Turner feud resulted in pitched battles in 1889 with the Turners successfully defending a siege of the courthouse. Fifty people are said to have died in the course of that feud.

The French-Eversale feud in Perry County led to a two-

49. The details of this feud and those described subsequently are from the studies done by Harrison and Klotter, pages 253-256.

day battle in the streets of Hazard which left nearly 50 dead and just as many orphans.

There are literally dozens more examples, but I will end this account with the most famous feud of all. The Hatfields and the McCoys feud, which commenced in the 1860s, pitted the Pike County, Kentucky, clan led by "Old Ran'l" McCoy against "Devil Anse" Hatfield, across the Tug Fork creek in West Virginia. Over some 30 years a modest (by feud standards) total of 12 to 20 Hatfields and McCoys were killed. But because of raids back and forth across state lines, governors became involved and a court case on the legalities of the raids went all the way to the United States Supreme Court. The national press had a field day, and it is likely most any literate person anywhere in the world would readily connect the mountains of Eastern Kentucky with the killings of the Hatfields and the McCoys. A stereotype was born, and survives to this day.

ASSASSINATION

The dominance of the regular rebel Democrats that occurred following the Civil War continued for three decades, but as is its wont, the Democratic Party developed factions over numerous issues. The splintering of the Democrats over the free silver issue in 1895 was so sharp that Kentucky elected its first Republican governor, William O. Bradley. The new division of power produced a stalemate in the election of a Senator by the General Assembly and helped in the election of William McKinley over William Jennings Bryan in the presidential election of 1896.

Amid all the confusion, William Goebel, son of a German immigrant, became a power in the Democratic Party. Part of his lustre came from his victory in a duel on the steps of the First National Bank in Covington in which he shot and killed John Sanford. Goebel's response to the Republican takeover of the Governor's office was the introduction of a bill in the Senate, "To Further Regulate Elections," which passed over the governor's veto and which set up a State Election Board to canvas election returns and settle disputes. The board had three members appointed by Goebel, two of whom naturally enough were Democrats, and thus Goebel had control.[50]

Goebel then ran for governor; at the Music Hall Convention in 1899 he out-maneuvered his two opponents and won the nomination. The general election that followed was between the Democrat, Goebel, the Republican, William S. Taylor, the People's Party, John G. Blair, and a bolted Democrat, John Y. Brown. William Jennings Bryan spoke in the state several times, on behalf of free silver, and on behalf of Goebel. The L&N Railroad directed its considerable clout against Goebel, and railroad employees, joined by many others, pushed out into the streets of Louisville causing a near civil war. The state militia was called out to patrol the polls on election day, and the official count gave Taylor, the Republican, the victory. Goebel Democrats quickly declared a controversy and called out the Goebel State Election Board to canvas the returns. The State Election Board actually decided the count for Taylor, but it was the General Assembly that would make the final decision.

The election challenge in the Capitol was extended for weeks and watched impatiently by hundreds of Eastern Kentucky Republicans brought to Frankfort by Caleb Powers, the Republican Secretary of State from Barbourville. The mountaineers with their guns surrounded the capitol building vowing not to let the Democrats steal away their victory. Unidentified Republicans were quoted as saying Goebel would never live to be inaugurated – and they were right. William Goebel was shot from a window in the Executive Office Building while approaching the state capitol. The General Assembly acted quickly, and threw out enough Republican votes for Goebel to

50. Clark, page 436.

be declared governor; he was given the oath of office, and died three days later.[51]

Kentucky now had two sets of Constitutional officers — the Republicans who had taken office after receiving a majority of the reported votes, and the Democrats, with young Lieutenant Governor J.C.W. Beckham taking Goebel's place, declared elected by the Democratic-controlled legislature. Most importantly, there were also two Adjutant Generals heading the Kentucky militia - General John Castleman, appointed by the Democrats, and General Daniel H. Collier, appointed by the Republicans.

It was widely assumed there would be war in Kentucky. The War Department in Washington was asked by Republican Governor Taylor to disarm the Democrats, but President McKinley declined to get involved in the "Kentucky Situation." There was one saving grace. The two Adjutant Generals, each with his own segment of loyal armed militia, were old friends and Masons together. They met and agreed not to start a war, but to let the courts and politics decide the issue. There, the Democrats had the advantage and ultimately won.

To this day it is uncertain who all the players were in the assassination plot. A man named Jim Howard was convicted of firing the shot, and Henry Yountsey, the secretary to Republican Governor Taylor, was convicted of complicity, but the Goebel Democrats made Republican Secretary of State, Caleb Powers, their major target. It was claimed the shot that killed Goebel came from Powers' office window, but the Secretary of State was out of town at the time.

Caleb Powers was tried four times for conspiring to murder William Goebel, and in the first three trials he was found guilty, and in the third he was sentenced to death by hanging and put on death row. In each trial the Democratic Judge and the prosecution were so overreaching that the Ken-

51. Samuel M. Wilson, *History of Kentucky, Vol. II*,(S.J. Clarke Publishing Co.) pages 539-562.

tucky Court of Appeals set aside the verdict and ordered a new trial. By the fourth trial many of the prosecution witnesses had admitted to perjury for money in the previous trials and were no longer useful, and the jury hung on the decision (11 to one for acquittal). Before Powers could be tried again a Republican was elected Governor and granted him a full pardon.

Powers had become so famous in his long court battles with the Democrats that he ran – and was easily elected – Congressman from Eastern Kentucky's Republican district. Kentucky is, I am confident, the only state in the union to boast a citizen sentenced to death by hanging, rising from the dark confines of death row to the marbled halls of the United States Congress.[52]

THE BLACK PATCH WAR

During the time of the political wars in Frankfort, a commercial war was brewing in Western Kentucky between the Black Patch farmers growing dark tobacco and the American Tobacco Company. Dark tobacco has a deep olive, almost ebony color to its leaf, quite different from the lighter burley that came later. Dark tobacco requires special care in cultivation and later in firing with smoke in the tobacco barns. Its texture and flavor make it most desirable for plug chewing tobacco, the most popular use for tobacco in the 1800s and early 1900s.

Buck Duke, son of George Washington Duke, the early North Carolina leader in tobacco manufacturing, took his father's early local successes and transformed them into a world-

52. Many authors have written of these events, including Caleb Powers autobiography written in prison, entitled, *My Own Story* (The Bobbs-Merrill Co., Indianapolis, 1905); James C. Klotter, William Goebel, *Politics of Wrath* (The University Press of Kentucky, 1977) and a book by Jim Short, the loquatious Mayor of Olive Hill, entitled, *Caleb Powers And the Mountain Army* (Jessica Publishing, Olive Hill, 1997).

wide trust that dominated the entire tobacco industry. He enjoyed making money and finding ways of taking over other companies, and discouraging competition. His growing monopoly became known as the Duke Trust. In the course of his adventures he managed to eliminate competitive bidding in the dark leaf tobacco auctions in Kentucky and Tennessee, and the price of tobacco fell from the traditional eight to twelve cents per pound to three cents. The cost to grow and fire a pound of tobacco was six cents.[53]

Financial ruin quickly descended on the Western Kentucky farmers. Bills couldn't be paid, notes were called, farms were lost, and there was no help from any source. This was the setting for the Black Patch War, which over a six-year period was truly a war in Western Kentucky. No one knows the number of killings, but clearly there was in this war more damage to property and more whippings than in the Civil War. It was a battle between the monopoly Duke trust from North Carolina and New York and the rural farmers of Kentucky and Tennessee.

It began on September 24, 1904, at a meeting in Guthrie, Kentucky, where hundreds of farmers, politicians, businessmen, and professionals and their families gathered to picnic, hear orations, and form The Dark Tobacco District Planters Association of Kentucky and Tennessee, thereafter known as the "Association." Congressman A.O. Stanley drew up many of the organization's legal documents, setting forth the clear object of the Association to pool all the dark tobacco production and hold it off the market until the Trust agents would meet the goal price of eight cents per pound.

To accomplish solidarity, Article 7 of the Association's Articles provided the members would "use influence and strong endeavor" to convince all tobacco farmers "to become members."

53. Bill Cunningham, *On Bended Knees* (McClanahan Publishing House, Inc., Nashville, Tenn., 1983), page 38.

The first year was slow going. The Trust adopted a policy of paying non-Association members twelve cents a pound and offering Association members nothing. Greed, and the natural independent attitude of Western Kentucky farmers to go it alone, made it very difficult for the Association.

By the second year the Association had signed up 70 percent of the growers but progress was still slow and conditions were critical. One individual who from the very first was drawn to the Association's cause was Dr. David Amoss, a family physician in Cobb, Kentucky. As unlikely as it may seem, he was a student, and became a master of military hit-and-run tactics. Dr. Amoss attended a meeting mostly of Tennessee Association members in October 1905 in the Stainback Schoolhouse in Robertson County, Tennessee, and there was born the "Possum Hunters," dedicated to convincing non-members the error of their ways.[54]

The Possum Hunters began by distributing handbills throughout the territory, and where that didn't work, they gave personal "lectures" in lonely places late at night — then whippings and finally the burning and scraping of tobacco plant beds.

Dr. Amoss went to Nashville to study tactics with the KKK, and borrowed ideas from other secret organizations.[55] He developed a military cadre of thousands of Western Kentucky farmers divided into lodges, coinciding with school districts, led by a "Captain," who reported to a "Colonel" presiding over a county, and in turn to "General" Amoss, who led the district. The men trained in night maneuvers, working in teams. They wore masks, and they wrapped their boots and their horses' hooves in burlap to avoid any sound. They became a proficient, integrated force.

As the late night raids by masked men began to receive notoriety, Congressman Stanley, in a speech, inadvertently labeled them the "Night Riders."

54. Ibid. page 53-54.

The expeditions grew ever larger and on the night of November 30, 1906, the town of Princeton, Kentucky, was invaded, occupied, and ransacked by an army of Night Riders. Squads of six men each stealthily slipped into town after midnight, captured the police station and disarmed the officers on duty, took over the telegraph and telephone offices, cut all outside communications, and occupied the fire station and cut its water supply. Simultaneously, 200 mounted men moved into town, patrolled the streets and shot at any house if a light went on. The major targets were the Orr Tobacco Factory and the Stagan & Dollar Warehouse. They were dynamited and torched to the ground, destroying 400,000 pounds of Trust tobacco in the process.

Upon a signal from their leader, General Amoss, the masked men gathered, their assignments completed, and rode out of town. Some terrified citizens, who opened their windows, heard the men singing as they departed, "The fires shine bright on my old Kentucky home..."

It was clear to everyone that Western Kentucky had a war, and it was soon known as the Black Patch War. The participants were both known and secret. Everyone knew who belonged to the Association, but the Night Riders wore masks. If you knew one, you pretended you didn't.

The night raids went on and on, and it became very difficult for any of the farmers to do business with the Trust, although some growers held out. The success at Princeton was so remarkable that Dr. Amoss and the other leaders began to plan for the big one — the Trust warehouses in Hopkinsville. The preparations were impossible to keep secret and the city fathers of Hopkinsville heard of the plans and prepared their defenses.

Only two people knew the actual date of the attack, and on November 19, 1907, all the forces assembled and were halfway to Hopkinsville when a spy reported the city had found out, and was prepared. Dr. Amoss pondered - they were so close - but he decided to call off the attack. The men quietly returned to their homes and the defenses, gathered in the city, waited all night in vain.

So, Hopkinsville's leaders relaxed, and on December 6, around 1 a.m., General Amoss and his troops slipped in and devastated the entire city. The method of infiltration, the capture of the police station, communications system, armory, and fire department, were the same techniques that were successful in Princeton. Even though Hopkinsville was a much larger city of 8,000 people the Night Riders were able to capture it lock, stock and barrel.

There were a number of people hurt and frightened almost to death, but no citizen of Hopkinsville was killed that night — which considering the rounds of ammunition fired — was a miracle. The pastor of the Methodist church heard the men, turned on his night light and looked out the window. A few minutes later, he counted 32 bullet holes in his room. The office of the city judge received 175 shots, and this was the pattern throughout the night.[56]

The Latham Warehouse, used by the Trust, was torched. The Tandy & Fairleigh Tobacco Factory was next. The Hopkinsville Kentuckian newspaper building was broken into and the paper's long-standing opposition to the Night Riders was repaid with the destruction of its presses with rifle shots and axes.

A buyer for the Trust, Lindsey Mitchell, was pulled from his home and struck repeatedly in the face with rifle butts and paraded through Hopkinsville as a bloody mess before being allowed to return home.

The job was completed; the destruction exceeded $200,000 and the Night Riders reassembled to start the journey home. Dr. Amoss, the General, was leading the way when

55. Bill Cunningham, *On Bended Knees* (McClanahan Publishing House Inc., Nashville, 1983) page 56.
56. Ibid. page 104.

he received a glancing bullet wound to the head from an unknown source. He was whisked away to receive treatment and recover from his wound. A hastily organized posse chasing the Night Riders caught up with one small group, and killed George Gray on his way home. The story of the Night Riders raid on Hopkinsville made headlines in The New York Times, and in major newspapers and journals throughout the country.

The Night Riders had their way, and the tobacco shortages they caused brought a rise in the price for dark leaf tobacco to the coveted eight cents a pound. The Association warehouses had all the business they could handle. The Association had won; it was time to end the war. But wars, once started, are hard to end, and this one continued for another three years with disastrous results.

Shortly following the Hopkinsville raid, a new governor was inaugurated, and he was Augustus E. Willson, a Republican from Louisville, a rich lawyer with connections to northern business interests, including the Duke Trust.

The Governor put state troops in Hopkinsville, Eddyville, Marion, Kuttawa, and in central Kentucky, with orders to stand guard, patrol the country roads, and break up any Association meetings.

Even so, the raids continued. Two warehouses were burned in Russellville in January 1908, and a house and tobacco factory burned in View, Kentucky shortly thereafter. On February 16, 1908, Eddyville was occupied at midnight and the masked men forced the owner of the hardware store out of bed and made him open up so the group could be re-supplied with buggy whips. Twelve men were selected and taken down by the river and whipped. Police Judge C. W. Rucker, a former city Marshall, and ten others suffered the licking of their lives. The inclusion of individuals uninvolved in the tobacco wars evidenced a blurring of the distinction between enemies of the Association and those considered "undesirables."

Often the occupying state troops made it difficult for

the Night Riders. Nevertheless, the raids, the burnings, the whippings continued, with a major difference. More often, there was a killing.

In the Eddyville raid, a group forced Henry Bennett, a businessman who dealt with the Trust, from his home and beat him so severely with kicks and whips and tree branches that he never recovered. On his headstone, his widow had inscribed: "Killed by the Night Riders." Many of the targets of the Night Riders packed up and left the state for good.

The situation grew more and more chaotic, and while General Amoss tried to lead, he had in fact, lost control.

Masked men, who may or may not have been Night Riders, made raids and burned and whipped to settle personal feuds. A force of more than 100 masked men invaded Birmingham in Marshall County and destroyed an entire black settlement, vowing "to run all the niggers out of Marshall County." In some places the Night Riders were called the "Negro chasers."

Dave Walker, a black man, was accused of cursing a white woman, and a masked mob set fire to his house. When he and his wife and his children ran out of the house, they were all killed by the mob.[57]

By this time everyone was sick of the violence and gradually the troops became more effective. Several brave victims of Night Rider beatings sued the Association leadership for damages in federal court and were successful. The Association members had to pay.

There was no doubt the Association had accomplished its goals. The Duke Trust was found guilty of monopoly in violation of the Sherman Anti-Trust law and was broken up. The price of tobacco rose in 1910 to a profitable twelve cents a pound.

Also in 1910, a grand jury indicted Dr. David Amoss,

57. Ibid. page 146.

and other leaders of the Association for the Hopkinsville raid. On March 6, the following year, he went on trial. There were turncoats to testify against him and the evidence mounted. At the end, Dr. Amoss took the stand, looked his peers on the jury in the eye, and swore he was not in Hopkinsville, but was tending a sick patient that night.

The jury was out for 40 minutes and returned with a verdict - "Not guilty."[58]

The Black Patch War was over.

LABOR WARS

One of the major common threads running through the scattered and varied peoples in Kentucky in the 19th century was the basic instinct of most for independence.

The coming of the industrial revolution drew many thousands of men and women from their farms and small stores into the regimented work in factories, mines, and railroads, causing a loss of this treasured independence, and ultimately, serious economic disadvantage. And thus arose the labor movement.

The struggle in Kentucky for a fair economic relationship between owner and worker has had its share of violent episodes and I will recount a few of the more robust and interesting, starting in the 1870s, the earliest days of the union movement.

The 1870s were one of the too-frequent periods of financial panic and depression in 19th century America, and a major area of economic problems was in the nation's railroads. Railroad strikes broke out in West Virginia, Pennsylvania, Ohio, Chicago, Saint Louis, and San Francisco during 1877, all protesting depressed wages and poor working conditions, and one leading to a bloody riot in Pittsburgh in July.

58. Ibid. pages 181-201.

There were severe problems in Kentucky as well, and when the L&N Railroad and the Short Line announced 10 percent wage reductions in the summer of 1877, a strike in Louisville was inevitable.

At this time a new force in the labor movement was emerging, called the Workingmen's Party U.S., an outgrowth of the revolutionary movement in Germany and founded on the teachings of Karl Marx. [59] The WPUS had a following in Louisville, principally within the immigrant population, and its members were active in the labor unrest of 1877.

Workers from the railroad companies gathered on July 22 to strike and protest, and they began a march through the city, picking up large numbers of unhappy and underpaid sewer construction workers along the way. The city's political and business leaders panicked at the news of the roving mob and gathered at City Hall where they had barricades erected, and messages sent to the capitol in Frankfort seeking troops and guns. The governor complied with 400 armed troops, and local officials enrolled an additional one thousand men into the militia.

The workers, meanwhile, gathered in the evening at City Hall and about 600 proceeded to march toward the railroad depot. Before long stones and bricks were being thrown at streetlights, and then at the freight depot, and finally along Broadway at the front windows of the homes of the wealthy denizens of the city.

Louis Brandeis, who was home from Harvard Law School, found his family's front window smashed, and he and his brother promptly went to City Hall, joined the militia, and began patrolling the streets with the others.[60]

59. Philip S. Foner, *The Great Labor Uprising of 1877* (Monad Press, New York, 1977), page 124 et seq.
60. Ibid. page 128. Brandeis later returned east for a remarkable career in the practice of law, and as Associate Justice of the United States Supreme Court. His papers and his remains are both at the University of Louisville, Brandeis School of Law.

When the mob reached the Short Line Depot they were met by 50 armed police who promptly opened fire, and the mob scattered. Three men were arrested, and it is not recounted how many men were hurt. Both the L&N and The Short Line rescinded their wage reductions.

During that same summer the Workingmen's Party was heavily involved in the election of state legislators. Over the vociferous objections of the city's businessmen and The Courier-Journal, which fumed about the "Red Menace," the WPUS was successful in electing five of the seven candidates.

The radical platform of the WPUS in those days called for: an eight-hour day; settlement of labor-management disputes by arbitration; prohibiting private firms from using prison labor; prohibiting child labor under age 14; compulsory education for children; lower taxes, and more economical government.

It would take over half a century for many of these goals to become a reality, and some we are still working on. The most famous of Kentucky's labor wars is undoubtedly the battle for unions in the coal mines of Harlan County. This is a battle that began in the early 1900s, and culminated in a nine-year stand off in the 1930s.

The key to the development of the Eastern Kentucky coal mines in the early 1900s was the railroad. In 1910, when Harlan County had no paved roads, a railroad spur was built into the county and three new mines produced 17,860 tons of coal in 1911 which was shipped out to the eastern markets. The annual tonnage expanded until 1928; almost 14 million tons were mined at a value of $25 million. Harlan ranked among the third or fourth wealthiest counties in Kentucky, although little of the wealth was owned by Kentuckians.[61]

The 1920s were booming times for Harlan County, and one of the records being set was for murders. Harlan

61. John W. Hevener, *Which Side Are You On?* (University of Illinois Press, Urbana, 1978), hereinafter referred to as Hevener, page 3.

County achieved a murder rate of 77.6 per 100,000 people. This was the highest murder rate of any one county in the United States, and at the time, was seven times the murder rate in Chicago, home of Al Capone and the Saint Valentine's Day Massacre.[62]

Historians and criminologists have pondered and written about the reasons for this phenomenon, and it is difficult to pinpoint. It was not a time of family feuds. Guns were very prevalent, but not dissimilar in number to the other mountain counties where murder rates were much lower. It was not a time of racial violence; Harlan County's black population was less than 10 percent of the total. It was not likely due to poverty, as these were relatively prosperous times.

Two theories, that tend to stick, point to Harlan County's poor level of education, with more than 12 percent illiteracy, and the disruptive nature of rapid industrialization and urbanization brought on by the development of the mines and the company towns. There was much stress in the lives of the miners and their families. Before industrialization, Harlan's murder rate was much lower, and it is much lower today. (During 1995, three murders were recorded in the county.)[63]

But as we approach the coal wars of the 1930s, the name "Bloody Harlan," was not the stuff of myth. It had been earned, as they say, the hard way.

The coming of the Great Depression of 1929, coupled with the economic disadvantage of the mountain coal fields, brought an end to Harlan County's prosperity. The coal operators in eastern Kentucky had difficulty competing under the best of conditions because of the differential freight costs to the eastern markets; and while Kentucky operators paid lower wages than their northern competitors, the softening demand for coal due to the national depression made profitable sales

62. Ibid. page 23.
63. Kentucky State Police Reports, *Crime In Kentucky*, 1995.

very difficult. The coal operator's solution was a further decrease in wages, and the battle for union organization took over.

There had been previous union activity in Harlan County abetted by the emergency conditions during World War I. The United Mine Workers (UMW) recruited 1,500 workers into three Union Locals, and there were some contracts signed during the war. Operators resisted whenever they could but the end of the war and government participation was the end of most of the leverage for the unions.

A national UMW strike in 1919 resulted in a Bituminous Coal Contract with substantial benefits for miners, but the Kentucky operators would not sign, and by 1924 Harlan county mines were entirely non-union.[64]

Organizers attempted to revive the UMW several times from 1926 and 1930 without much success. Many of the miners were hesitant about the union. They did not think of themselves as a group of workers with common interests. They still thought of themselves as independent mountain men, looking to their families and the old independent ways.

In the instances where the union was making headway, the coal operators with their private mine guards, and in league with the County Sheriff and other county officials, ran the organizers off and fired any miner openly sympathetic to the union cause. Being fired meant not only the loss of a job but the immediate eviction of the family from the company-owned home. This was serious leverage.

The Harlan County Coal Operators Association was officially formed in 1916, and included all the major coal mines except U.S. Coal & Coke and Wisconsin Steel, and was a major military and political force throughout the conflict. The leaders of the Association were either major Republican or

64. Hevener, page 6. James C. Klotter's, *Kentucky: Portrait in Paradox, 1900-1950*, (Kentucky Historical Society, Frankfort, Kentucky, 1996) is also an excellent source of material on the coal wars of Harlan County, pages 139-143.

major Democratic state figures, depending on how the political winds were blowing.

From 1929 to 1931 employment in the mines dropped by 10 percent, days worked were decreased, and average earnings of a miner fell from $1,235 to $749 a year.

The conditions were bad, and while most miners could still buy food and stay warm, that was about it. There was increasing evidence of malnutrition, particularly among the children.

On February 16, 1931, the Coal Operators announced a 10 percent wage reduction and the long union war began. William Turnblazer, a union man, said, "We might as well die fighting, as die of starvation."[65]

But starvation set in, and for the first time in Harlan County's history the county appealed for outside help. The American Red Cross responded, however, it would only provide relief to those who suffered from a recent drought. Coal miners didn't qualify.[66]

On Sunday, March 1,1931, more than 2,000 Harlan and Bell County miners attended a rally in Pineville to hear UMW Vice President Phillip Murray urge them to organize and cooperate, but "not to precipitate strikes or create an industrial catastrophe."[67] The coal operators had spies at the meeting taking down names, and the next day the Harlan-Wallins Coal Corp. dismissed 49 employees; Black Star, 60; and Black Mountain Coal Corp., more than 165. All were from the spies' list.

As the hunger grew, the looting began. The A&P at Evarts was cleaned out on April 23, the East Harlan Coal Company's commissary on April 24, John Powell's grocery was looted on April 29, and on it went. Appeals were made to Frankfort, Congress and to President Hoover, but there was

65. Hevener, page 14.
66. Ibid. page 33.
67. Ibid. page 33.

little response.

The United States District Court did act, however, on the petition of the Black Mountain Coal Company. The Court entered a restraining order on April 25, prohibiting any of the UMW field representatives from entering company property or talking to or in any way influencing company employees to strike. Thus, the union was rendered powerless to organize.

The miners were also faced daily with the harassment of the mine company guards. The guards were appointed deputy sheriffs under the command of sheriff John Henry Blair, but they were paid by the coal operators, and by all accounts were a pretty despicable lot. At one time in the '30s, it was documented that of the 169 deputies, 64 had been indicted and 27 convicted of felonies. Eight of those were for manslaughter and three for murder.

To add salt to the miners' wounds, the deputies were paid twice as much by the operators as the average $75 earned a month by miners.[68] It was these deputies who evicted the miners from the company houses, who ran off the organizers, and treated all miners as the enemy. As one miner's wife described it, "The law is a gun thug in a big automobile."[69]

The friction between the miners and the gun thugs escalated, and there were shootings. A night watchman was wounded by a sniper hiding in the woods. Three deputies fired on a miner who returned the fire, killing one.

On April 27, a dynamite blast destroyed a mine entry at Shields, and subsequently 50 discharged union miners fired on non-union miners on their way to work. At Caywood, 16 company houses where miners had been evicted were torched. On May 5, a coal company caravan of non-union miners and deputies was ambushed by approximately 60 union men at a cut in the road several hundred yards below Evarts. Hundreds

68. George T. Blakey, *Hard Times and New Deal in Kentucky* (The University Press of Kentucky, Lexington, 1986),hereinafter referred to as Blakey, page 162.
69. Ibid. page 40.

of rounds of gunfire were exchanged in the next half-hour, killing and wounding a half dozen men. For days thereafter a state of anarchy reigned in Evarts, with sporadic shootings. The schools were closed, and many families fled.[70]

One result of the Evarts war was that all the miners throughout the county went on strike, and despite the prevalent hunger the grievance voiced the loudest was against the gun thug deputies. When news of the war reached Frankfort, Governor Sampson dispatched troops to bring order.

The troops came in, the governor made promises to the miners, but besides the restoration of order not much changed.

The UMW was broke, was unable to assist with food relief for the miners, and its leaders gave up on organizing the mines. The deputy guards stayed on, the mines offered work at the reduced rate to non-union miners, and the workers either accepted or left the county.

Florence Reece's husband, Sam, was a union man and after their house was raided and Sam run off, she wrote this ballad on the back of a calendar, her only paper:

"With pistols and with rifles
They take away our bread
And if you miners hinted it
They'll sock you on the head.
    Which side are you on?
    Which side are you on?
Gentlemen, can you stand it?
Oh, tell me how you can?
Will you be a gun thug
Or will you be a man?
    Which side are you on?
    Which side are you on?

70. Ibid. page 45.

> If you go to Harlan County
> There is no neutral there
> You'll either be a union man
> Or a thug for J.H. Blair.
>   Which side are you on
>   Which side are you on."[71]

In June 1933, Congress passed the National Industrial Recovery Act which in Section 7 guaranteed workers the right to join a union and bargain collectively, and the UMW, now under the leadership of John L. Lewis, started a comeback. The UMW first organized the miners in Bell County and used that base to make inroads into Harlan County. In short order they recruited 5,000 miners and after a three-week strike the operators signed a one-year contract. But this did not mean that the operators were about to give up.

The mine guards continued to resist union organizers, union men were ambushed, and non-union men were fired on in return. In November 1934, union organizers were denied rooms at the New Harlan Hotel, because the proprietor wisely feared reprisals from "the biggest gang of dynamiters on earth." In February 1935, Governor Laffoon appointed a commission, headed by Adjutant General Henry Denhardt, to investigate the trouble in Harlan County. After investigation, the Commission reported to the Governor:

> there exists a virtual reign of terror, financed in general by a group of coal mine operators in collusion with certain public officials; the victims of this reign of terror are the coal miners and their families ... free speech and the right of peaceable assemblage is scarcely tolerated. Those who attend meetings are promptly discharged and evicted from their

71. Ibid. page 61. Also, Klotter, *Kentucky: Portrait in Paradox, 1900-1950*, page 141. This is one of many labor songs later made famous by Woody Guthrie.

homes. Many are beaten and mistreated in most unjust and un-American methods by some operators using so-called "peace officers" to carry out their desires.[72]

But no action was taken, and when the Supreme Court declared the National Industrial Recovery Act unconstitutional later in 1935, the operators promptly returned to non-union operations.

A new Act, The National Labor Relations Act (The Wagner Act) was passed by Congress in 1935, once again giving workers the right to organize and bargain collectively. With this news, the Harlan County miners gathered on Sunday, July 7, 1935, at Evarts to celebrate and talk about organizing. Quickly, deputies shut off the road into Evarts preventing many miners and union leaders from reaching the rally, while other deputies drove past the meeting blowing their car horns so the speakers couldn't be heard. A fight started with the deputies, shots were fired and the meeting was disbanded.

The deputies ruled. The operators declared the Wagner Act would not change the non-union operations of the mines; again the organizers lost, and again they left.

It wasn't until 1937 that the UMW decided to try it again and 15 union recruiters were sent to Harlan where this time they were successful in getting rooms at the New Harlan Hotel. Shortly thereafter, three stench bombs were detonated in the hotel hallways and all the hotel occupants were forced out into the streets to witness dynamite bombs destroying the union organizers' automobiles.

On Sunday afternoon, January 31, 1937, snipers fired on union representative Marshall Musick and his wife walking back from church. A week later, six organizers returning from a Black Mountain meeting were ambushed and one was

72. Blakey, page 114.

seriously wounded. While Musick was on an organizing trip to Pineville, three cars full of men stopped in front of his small house and fired volleys of bullets, killing their teen-age son, Bennett, who was standing in his living room.

These latest acts of violence resulted in no indictments, but they did make national headlines. The combination of national attention and the shocked reaction of the community to the death of a young boy shot in his own living room, may well be what set Harlan County on the road to recovery. There was more violence yet to come, but the forces of reason were on the rise.

National attention centered on the U.S. Senate Sub-Committee, known as the LaFollette Civil Liberties Committee, headed by Senator Robert Lafollette of Wisconsin. The Committee investigated violations of labor's civil liberties by employers fighting unionization, and now focused its attention on Harlan County.

The publicity brought on by the Lafollette hearings resulted in United States Department of Justice prosecutions against operators and deputies for conspiring to violate the Wagner Act, and in six successful union elections supervised by the National Labor Relations Board. By August 1937, the UMW had successfully recruited over 9,000 (65 percent) of the Harlan County miners.

There were more hurdles. The first was obtaining union contracts with the major mine owners. By this time almost all the mines in the country were union, except in Harlan County, and the continued resistance there was an economic threat to all. Negotiations in the spring of 1937 were not going well, but for the first time a split developed in the solidarity of the Coal Operators Association, and a number of operators pulled out. The union had success with the non-member firms and by the end of that year, 6,000 county miners had UMW agreements.

The remaining members of the Coal Operators Association responded by setting up their own company unions and continuing with violent reprisals against union miners. The UMW answered by filing charges with the National Labor Relations Board against 27 Harlan companies for unfair labor practices. In addition, the United States Justice Department investigated coal operators activities and a Federal Grand Jury returned indictments against 22 coal companies, 24 coal operators, Harlan county sheriff Middleton, and 22 deputies for conspiring to deprive miners of their civil rights. During the course of these proceedings one defendant, Frank White, was murdered before he could testify, and the man charged with the crime, Chris Patterson, was murdered after being released on bond.

With these killings the violence had almost run its course, and the accumulating pressures of the federal government and the local union brought the coal operators to end the holdout and sign union contracts.

But there was a second and final hurdle. John L. Lewis of the UMW was worried about competition from the rival Progressive Mine Workers Union of the AFL, and started a drive for a closed shop; that is, an agreement in his contracts that requires all workers to belong to the UMW.

This was difficult, particularly in independent-minded Harlan, but the UMW began a national shutdown to obtain a union shop. After four weeks of the strike the vast majority of the nation's operators signed union shop agreements, then in time others signed, until Harlan County operators stood alone in opposition. But the miners now were united and when the national strike was called every mine in Harlan County was shut down. This was a first, but it wouldn't be the last.

As the strike in Harlan County wore on some mines opened and tried to operate with non-union miners or union miners willing to cross a picket line. Each time, the strikers would converge on the mine and do whatever was necessary to close it. They blocked roads, cut telephone lines, threatened strike breakers, smashed windows, surrounded buildings and held operators hostage - whatever it took.

The operators responded by going to Frankfort seeking help from Governor Albert B. "Happy" Chandler, who was on record as opposing closed union shops. Because of the violence and the threat of violence, Governor Chandler dispatched several hundred Kentucky National Guardsmen to occupy Harlan County and allow the operators to reopen the mines without a contract. The troops arrived and took their positions on May 15, 1939.

Many of the operators opened their mines with as many workers as they could get, and the UMW worked to keep discipline among the strikers and to avoid confrontations with the National Guard. The troop strength was increased to 1,250. [73]

When the strike was in its fifteenth week the UMW held a mass meeting on Sunday, and the leaders called for picketing the open mines, and on Monday picketing began at five mines. There was considerable pentup frustration on all sides, and at the Mahan-Ellison mine at Stanfill a fight erupted between the pickets and the National Guard. A picket tried to halt the mine trolley, and Captain Hanbery of the Guard tried to stop him, and was shot in the stomach. The captain, though wounded, drew his revolver and opened fire on the picket line, and everybody started shooting. Five picketers were seriously wounded and two died. Two soldiers were hurt.

Two hundred and twenty seven union members were arrested on the spot and marched nine miles to the Harlan County jail. As the prisoners marched up Main Street in Harlan, a miner's mother protesting the arrest of her son was shot in the leg. Five hundred more Guardsmen, this time with tanks, were rushed in, but now the violence was over.

The operators and union representatives resumed negotiations, this time with a personal message from Secretary of

73. Ibid. page 164.

Labor Frances Perkins demanding that they resolve the matter. Roosevelt sent his administration's top industrial trouble shooter, John Steelman. When negotiations again deadlocked, Dr. Steelman moved in with a plan that the union accepted, and after two days of agonizing, the operators finally accepted. A contract was signed on July 19; the strike, nine years of turmoil, suffering and violence, were over.

In the many years since, the coal industry has had its ups and downs, as has the UMW, and there have been disputes and strikes, but in these labor wars there have been no more killings. Bloody Harlan is now history.

RACE WARS

We noted that race was not a factor in the Harlan County labor wars, but there has been racial violence throughout Kentucky's history, some of which I have recounted in earlier sections. Most of these events were white men's violence against blacks. Looking to more recent examples of violence in Kentucky, I find instances when the angry mob was black, and one of those times was May 27, 1968, in Louisville.

Following the assassination of Dr. Martin Luther King on April 14, 1968, Kentucky shared the national mourning, and busloads of Kentuckians traveled to Atlanta for his funeral. The following Sunday, a memorial service, attended by hundreds, was held on the steps of the court house in Louisville. Not long thereafter a white police officer was accused of using excessive force in arresting a black man. This was not a rare event, and it added to the frustrations of the black community concerned with jobs, housing, school discriminations, the murder of Dr. King, and an often expressed sense of powerlessness in the greater community.

A rally to protest police brutality was held on Monday evening, May 27, at the intersection of 28th and Greenwood, and the scheduled speaker was Stokely Carmichael. He did not arrive, however, and other speakers took his place. An assistant to Stokely Carmichael reportedly told the large crowd that the "honkeys" (whites) had kept Carmichael's plane from landing.

When the rally was over, the crowd began to disperse, and all seemed normal enough until three city police cars pulled into the intersection to help clear it out. Spectators reported a group of young kids, between the ages of 11 and 15, started throwing rocks at the police cars.[74]

The police radioed for help, and as more police cars arrived the anger of the crowd crescendoed into a riot that rocked the city for the better part of three days and nights. From the center at 28th and Greenwood, the crowd — besieged by police — broke into roving bands and spread out in all directions, leaving fires, overturned cars, broken windows and looted stores in their wake.

When the city police ran out of cars, the county police units were called in, and then the Kentucky State Troopers (141 men), and finally the National Guard (1000 men). Governor Louie Nunn came to Louisville to confer with Mayor Kenneth Schmied.

The Mayor proclaimed a curfew, and things calmed down somewhat, but then mobs gathered again sporadically on Tuesday, Wednesday and Thursday. The police and troops patrolled, and rushed from one place to another as violence was reported. Roving bands came to Fourth Street, still a major shopping district, and after some damage was done, police closed Fourth Street from Broadway to River Road, and set up guards. The Bank of Louisville Branch at 28th and Dumesnil came under siege until police arrived and rescued the bank employees huddled in a rear room.

74. These accounts of the riot are taken from news reports in *The Courier-Journal*, for Tuesday, May 28 through Friday, May 31, 1968, and the *Report of the Louisville Human Relations Commission*, 1968, and *The Way It Is*, transcript of WHAS-TV news program, May 29, 1968.

Hundreds of incidents were reported, hundreds of black men and boys were arrested, hundreds of thousands of dollars of damage was done, much of it in the black community. The police occasionally fired their guns, and two young black men were killed while many, many more were wounded and injured.

The anger and the energy finally ran its course. The troops went home and there was a great mess to be cleaned up. There was much talk about the need for better communication between the white power structure and the black community, and steps were taken to make open housing a reality and to address some of the other inequities. That struggle continues to this day.

CHILDREN

It has been a long time since we've had a lynching, "Regulators" riding into town to keep people in line, or angry mobs protesting monopoly trusts by burning and killing. These are things of Kentucky's past.

We have developed a criminal justice system that is run by professionals and enforces our laws. When the system breaks down we have meetings and protests and people are fired, or not re-elected, and laws are changed. Individual and collective violent action to enforce a public code of order, which was long a major characteristic of Kentucky life, is past.

We say of ourselves, in criticism, that we have become a litigious society, quick to file a law suit, and that is true. That is one of the ways we have ended the duels and ambushes and feuds of a few generations ago.

We will never be a society without tensions and conflict, but we have learned much about easing those tensions and resolving the conflicts without bloodshed. But we still have a ways to go. Violence is still on our minds, and is still a problem. Even though the number of violent crimes has decreased significantly in the last 30 years,[75] we are still accosted daily with newspaper and television reports of violence. And of most concern recently, is the killing of children by children.

In 1993, in Grayson, Kentucky, Scott Pennington, who was a senior at East Carter High School, took his English class captive, and shot and killed his teacher and a custodian. Four years later, on December 1, 1997, 14-year-old Michael Carneal at Heath High School in Paducah fired nine or ten bullets into a student prayer group, killing three classmates and wounding five.[76]

In 1997, there were children shooting children at four schools in Oregon, Arkansas, Mississippi — in addition to Kentucky — resulting in 12 deaths and 47 wounded.

The statistics: There were five children with guns in the four school shootings. The five were all boys, they were all white, and 41 of the 59 shot were female. All of the victims were white.

The father of one of the young girls killed at Heath High School in Paducah, said: "There is ... a lot of pain and a lot of tears. The obvious question for us is, Why?"

We don't know why. We do know that children get lonely and frightened and depressed, and can be as mentally ill as grown-ups.

We need to know why. We need to spend the time and resources to do better for our children, and we must ask ourselves in our concern for our children, what role does the death penalty play in this? Should we execute our children who kill? Does the fact that the state kills affect our children?

We do currently kill our children if they've reached the age of 16 when they kill. And we must know in our hearts that when children see the state killing, they are affected by it.

75. See Kentucky State Police Report, *Crimes in Kentucky* , set forth in Chapter 3, Section 1, "Deterrence."
76. The information on incidence of school violence is taken from a series in *The Courier-Journal*, December 6-8, 1998, by C. Ray Hall, and other staff writers.

The state executed Harold McQueen, with enormous publicity, at Eddyville on July 1, 1997. Michael Carneal took a gun into nearby Heath High School and fired on his class-mates five months later on December 1, 1997. The execution clearly was not a deterrent in that case. We must wonder what damage it did to our children.

Since our first experience of violence in Kentucky in 1742, our people have braved the frontier, survived the internecine lunacy of the Civil War and met the social up-heavals of the industrial revolution. We have faced and struggled to overcome racial prejudices and taken on the difficulties of an increasingly urban society and the needs of our people for education and economic opportunity. We have accomplished much.

In reviewing this history, it is apparent that no matter how wild our excesses, how idiotic our fringes, we continually wished to do better for our own lives and those who would follow, and we have. There are no more guerrillas, nor vigilan-tes, nor lynchings, nor feud killings. The number of homi-cides continues to decrease. We are becoming a less violent society and yet we retain the anachronism of the death penalty.

In the chapters that follow, we will review the history of the death penalty in Kentucky, and then consider the argu-ments presented in support of the death penalty, and answer them one by one.

We will see that executions serve no purpose and are only a reminder of our violent past.

CHAPTER II
A BRIEF HISTORY OF THE LAWS
OF CAPITAL PUNISHMENT

"the last melancholy resource"

The many occasions of violence we covered in our brief history of violence often had political origins, and frequently had political ramifications reflected in Kentucky's often-amended death penalty laws. A review of the history of these laws will be another step in our understanding of where we have been and where we should be going.

When Kentucky separated from Virginia and became the fifteenth state in the Union, on June 1, 1792, our first Constitution provided in Article VIII (6):

"All laws now in force in the State of Virginia not inconsistent with this Constitution, which are of a general nature, and not local to the eastern part of the state, shall be in force in this State until they shall be altered or repealed by the Legislature."

At that time the Virginia criminal laws, reflecting the harsh English laws, mandated the death sentence for all convicted murderers,[1] and imposed the death penalty for a wide range of other offenses. England's criminal laws came to be known as the bloody code — as many as 200 crimes were punishable by death — including pick-pocketing, shoplifting, steal-

---

1. See the discussion in *McGautha v. California*, 402 U.S.183, 198, 91 S.Ct. 1454,1462, (1971) and *Furman v. Georgia*, 408 U.S. 238, 246, 92 S.Ct. 2726, 2730 (1972). The opinions note there was a rebellion against this Common Law rule almost from the beginning of our country, resulting in legislation restricting the death penalty in the states, and a widespread reluctance of juries to convict on capital offenses.

ing turnips, and associating with gypsies.[2]

Virginia's code of criminal law was not well accepted in Kentucky, particularly the multiple offenses punishable by death, and when the newly elected Legislature first turned its attention to the criminal statutes in 1798, it provided:

"No crime whatsoever, committed by any free person against the Commonwealth (except murder of the first degree) shall be punished with death, within the same."

The Preamble to this Act of 1798 gives a keen insight into the minds and hearts of early Kentuckians on the subject of crime and punishment, and I quote it in its entirety (the emphases are mine):

"WHEREAS it frequently happens that wicked and dissolute men, resigning themselves to the dominion of inordinate passions, commit violations on the lives, liberties, and property of others; and the secure enjoyment of these having principally induced men to enter into society, government would be defective in its principal purpose, were it not to restrain such criminal acts, by inflicting due punishment on those who perpetrate them; but it appears at the same time equally deducible, from the purposes of society, that a member thereof committing an inferior injury, does not wholly forfeit the protection of his fellow citizens, but after suffering punishment in proportion to his offense, is entitled to protection from all greater suffering; so that it becomes a duty in the legislature, to arrange in a proper scale the crimes which it may be necessary for them to repress, and to adjust thereto a corresponding gradation of punishments. And, *whereas the reformation of offenders, an object highly meriting the attention of the laws, is not effected at all by capital punishments, which exterminate instead of reforming, and should be the last melancholy resource against those whose existence is become inconsistent with the safety of their fellow citizens; which also weaken the state by cutting off so many, who, if reformed, might be restored sound members to society, who, even under a course of labor might be rendered useful to the community, and who would be living and long continued examples, to deter others from committing the like offenses.* And forasmuch as experience in all ages and countries hath shewn that cruel and sanguinary laws defeat their own purpose, by engaging the benevolence of mankind to withhold prosecutions, to smother testimony, or to listen to it with bias; and by producing in many instances total dispensation and impunity, under the names of pardon and benefit of clergy; when if the punishment were only proportioned to the injury, men would feel it their inclination, as well as their duty, to see the laws observed; for rendering crimes and punishments therefore more proportionate to each other."[3]

We see in the rough and tumble times of our early statehood, when much of Kentucky was still a frontier of hardships and dangers, the people's representatives expressing concern with the fairness of punishments and the rehabilitation of the wayward. The "last melancholy resource" of the death penalty was only to occur if the criminal was beyond reformation and society could not otherwise be protected.

From this initial minimalist philosophy our legislature has wandered up and down the scales of violent punishments, reflecting the passions and fears of the times, with the most notable surges occurring in response to the violence of the Civil War, the fears of whites of freed slaves after the war, and the 20th century industrial age crowding of the poor and under-employed, festering crime and violence in urban centers.

The early phase of restricted capital punishment applied only to whites. Blacks were treated much differently. For example, only three years after the Preamble and restrictive statute cited above, the Kentucky legislature provided:

"Be it further enacted, that any slave or slaves, free negro or mulatto, hereafter duly convicted of voluntary manslaughter, shall suffer death.[4]

"Be it further enacted, that any slave or slaves hereafter duly convicted of an attempt to commit a rape on the body

2. William O. Reichert, "Capital Punishment Reconsidered," 47 *Kentucky Law Journal* No. 3, page 398, discusses the history of capital punishment in England.
3. Acts of 1798, January Session, Chapter IV, Sec. 1.
4. Digest of the Statute Laws of Kentucky, Morehead & Brown, Vol. II, page 1288.

of any white woman such slave or slaves so convicted shall suffer death."

In 1819:

"Be it enacted by the General Assembly of the Commonwealth of Kentucky, that if any slave shall willfully and maliciously shoot at any free white person, with a gun or other instrument, with intent to kill such person; or if any slave shall willfully and maliciously wound any free white person, with intent to kill such person, the slave so offending, his or her aider, abettors and counsellors, being a slave or slaves, shall be held guilty of felony, and shall thereafter suffer death."

In 1830, construction for the Louisville and Portland Canal, designed to bypass the rapids of the Ohio, began. When it was completed in 1833 the Legislature (for reasons or threats now unknown) made it a specific crime "to blow up, or attempt to blow up, with gunpowder, any of the locks of the Louisville and Portland Canal."

If one were convicted, and one were white, the penalty was two to four years in the penitentiary. But Section 3 of the Act provided:

"Be it further enacted, That each and every slave who shall commit ... the offenses aforesaid, shall be guilty of felony, and upon being convicted thereof, shall suffer death by hanging."[5]

By the early 1850s the Commonwealth's laws on capital punishment for whites had also broadened. In addition to murder in the first degree, additional crimes punishable by death were treason and statutory rape of a child under 12.

Also, the legislature in 1852 enacted a statute providing:

"If any free white person advise, counsel or conspire with a negro, bond or free, and cause him to rebel or make insurrection against the authority of his master or the laws of the land, he shall be punished with death, or confinement in the penitentiary not less then six nor more then ten years, at

5. Ibid. page 1304.

the discretion of the jury."[6]

The coming struggles of the Civil War were foreshadowed by our legislators. The method of execution, from the earliest days, was hanging, and the statutes provided:

"Persons sentenced to suffer death shall be hung by the neck until dead, at such time and place as the court shall order, by the sheriff of the county, or other person designated by the court. The time fixed for the execution of the sentence shall not be less then twenty nor more then ninety days, unless the public peace and safety, in the opinion of the court, require a shorter time."[7]

Records of state executions no longer exist, if they ever did, for the period 1792 to 1870. Those 78 years of our history of executions are not documented. But starting in 1871, there are records that are noted as we proceed.[8] In the decade of 1871 to 1880 there were eight state executions by hanging, and of those, six were black men. The offenses were murder (6) and rape (2). This is an average of less then one execution a year. These statistics, and none of those that follow, include any of the mob lynching and vigilante killings that occurred outside the law.

In the aftermath of the Civil War and the pervasive violence of the reconstruction era, public hangings, particularly of blacks, became to many an embarrassing public spectacle, drawing increasing attention and criticism both locally and nationally. In 1893, the legislature responded by amending the hanging statute: "... the execution shall take place in some enclosure convenient to the prison where the defendant is confined, in the presence of not more then fifty persons, ten of whom may be designated by the court rendering the judgment, and the remainder by the sheriff executing it. No

6. *The Revised Statutes of Kentucky*, Turner & Nicholas, 1852, Art. III, page 247, Art. IV, page 248.
7. Ibid. Art. I, Sec. 20, page 246.
8. Execution data for the period May 1872 to July 1911, is taken from Appendix B of *Racial Violence in Kentucky*, 1865-1940 by George C. Wright, (Louisiana State University Press, Baton Rouge) 1990.

fee shall be charged to any person permitted to witness the execution."[9]

In addition to the problems of vigilante hangings there was the danger of vigilante rescues. The legislature addressed this danger in 1893:

"If in any county of this commonwealth there is no jail, or the same is insecure, or there is danger or probable danger, that any person confined therein...will be rescued therefrom by violence, the judge of the circuit court for said county shall ... direct that such person be transferred to the jail of the nearest county in which the jail is secure ..."[10]

By 1893 life imprisonment became an alternative to execution for first degree murder. Forcible rape of a woman over 12 was decreed a capital crime punishable by death; an alternative sentence of ten to 20 years in the penitentiary was available to the sentencing jury. Most often it was the convicted black man who received death, and his white counterpart the lesser sentence.

Also in 1893, burning a house, in whole or in part, within the walls of a penitentiary was also deemed a capital crime.

From 1881 to 1910, there were 97 state executions (53 black men and 44 white men). Of those executed, 84 were charged with murder and 13 charged with rape. This is an average of one execution every four months, and 54 percent of those executed were black. The 1900 census reported the black population of Kentucky at 7.5 percent.

In the late 1800s, there was a growing unease with hanging as the method of execution in Kentucky. The process was easily botched if the rope were too long or too short, and the results generally were gruesome. With the developing science of electricity came the movement for electrocution as the method of killing, and in 1910 the Kentucky legislature went modern:

9. *The Revised Statutes of Kentucky*, Turner & Nicholas, Section 44, page 767.
10. Russell, *Statutes of Kentucky*, 1909, Art. 39, page 897.

Section 1. "That from and after the period that this law shall take effect the mode of the execution of a death sentence must in every case be by causing to pass through the body of the condemned a current of electricity of sufficient intensity to cause death as quickly as possible, and the application of such current must be continued until the condemned is dead. All executions of the death penalty by electrocution shall take place within the walls of the state penitentiary, hereafter indicated by the Board of Prison Commissioners, and in such enclosure as will exclude public view thereof."[11]

But the mores of Kentucky hangings, particularly the hanging of a black man accused of raping a white woman, were too strong, and just ten years later in 1920 the legislature amended the mandatory electric chair law by adding:

"Except in cases where the accused has been adjudged to suffer a death sentence for the crime of rape or attempted rape, in which event sentence shall be executed by hanging the condemned in the county in which the crime was committed. The sentence to be executed by the sheriff of the county." [12]

In that same legislative session in 1920 the representatives took note again of the continuing problem of vigilantes and lynch mobs. Chapter 41, Section 1, page 187 provides:

"Any number of persons more than three, assembled for the purpose of doing violence, injury to, or lynching any person in custody of any peace officer or jailer in this Commonwealth, shall be regarded as a mob. Any person who takes part in and with any such mob, with the result that the person in custody meets death at the hands of any such mob shall be deemed guilty of lynching, or if the result be that the person does not meet death, any person who takes part in or with the mob shall be guilty of attempted lynching.

"The penalty for lynching shall be death or life imprisonment."

In the decade 1911 to 1920, there were 36 executions,

11. Kentucky Acts, 1910, Chapter 38, Sec. 1, page 111.
12. Kentucky Acts, 1920, Chapter 163, page 693.

an average slightly higher than one every four months. Twenty-six of the men executed were black (72 percent) and ten were white (28 percent).

Beyond the worries about blacks and mob violence, there was in 1920 a new threat — the communists taking over Kentucky. The legislature addressed this perceived threat by passing "criminal syndicalism" and "sedition" laws. Criminal syndicalism was defined as violently bringing about political revolution, and sedition was suggesting by "word, act, deed, or writing" public disorder to overthrow the Kentucky government. If a violation of this act resulted in the death of any person, the punishment was death, or confinement in the state penitentiary for life.[13]

In 1928, the new capital offense of kidnapping, was added by the legislature:

"Any person or persons who forcibly or otherwise holds any person against his or her will for the purpose of unlawfully obtaining a ransom for the release of such person...shall, on conviction thereof, be deemed guilty of a felony and punished by confinement in the state penitentiary for life, or by death, in the discretion of the jury."[14]

Assault with intent to rob was also made a capital crime:

"If any person, with an offensive weapon or instrument, shall unlawfully and maliciously assault, or in or by any forceable and violent manner, demand any money, goods, or chattels, bond, bill, deed, or will, or other evidence of right, or other thing of value of or from any other person, with an intent to rob or commit a robbery upon such person, he shall be guilty of a felony and upon conviction shall be punished by confinement in the state penitentiary for twenty one years, or for life, or by death, in the discretion of the jury."[15]

Juries did not pay much attention to the expanded death sentences, with the sole exception of the case of Sam

13. Kentucky Acts, 1920, Chapter 100, Section 8. The Sedition Act was later held unconstitutional in *Braden v. Commonwealth*, Ky., 291 SW2d 843 (1956).
14. Kentucky Acts, 1928, Chapter 42, page 178.
15. Kentucky Acts, 1934, Chapter 51, Sec. 1160.

Franklin, a black man from Jefferson County. Sam Franklin was executed in 1937 for armed robbery, the only execution during this period for a crime other than murder or rape. The total figures for 1921 through 1939 are 79 executions, of which 35 were black men (44 percent) and 44 white men (56 percent). Besides the one armed robbery execution, there were 76 for murder and two for rape. The number of executions for this period is significantly higher than the earlier periods, with an average of more then one every three months.

In the 1940s there were 34 executions, of which sixteen were white men (47 percent), and eighteen were black men (53 percent). From 1950 until the execution of Kelly Moss in 1962 (the last execution until 1997), there were seventeen executions, of which eight were white men (47 percent), and nine were black men (53 percent). The flow of executions had slowed to an average of well under two a year.[16]

A bill to abolish the death penalty (H.B. 229) was introduced in the 1958 General Assembly, and I mark that as the beginning of the modern abolition movement. While the bill was pending a large number of letters to the editor appeared in the Kentucky press venting hostility to the abolition proposal. The bill was easily defeated, and none of this is news, except that the occurrence caused an assistant professor of political science at the University of Kentucky, William O. Reichert, to publish an article in the Kentucky Law Journal entitled, "Capital Punishment Reconsidered."[17]

This, to my knowledge, is the first comprehensive polemic for the abolition of the death penalty published in Kentucky since the adoption of the Preamble to the Criminal Jus-

16. The execution data from 1911 to 1962 is from "Legal Electrocutions at the Kentucky State Penitentiary Since July 8, 1911," vertical files archives, Kentucky Department for Libraries and Archives, Frankfort, Ky. There are discrepancies between these records and those cited in Note 8, where they overlap. The earlier records include 10 additional executions of nine blacks and one white, which I have not included.
17. *Kentucky Law Journal*, Vol. 47, No. 3, (Spring 1959), page 397, hereinafter referred to as Reichert.

tice Act of 1798.[18]

Professor Reichert commences:

"The popular notion that the penalty of death is the most efficient, if not the only, means of deterring murder has become so deeply embedded in the folklore of American society that it is rarely evaluated as to its basic validity.

" ... Capital punishment, if it is to be defended successfully, must be proven to be adequate in two particulars. Not only must it be shown that the immediate and practical effect of the death penalty is to deter the murderer from committing an isolated act of violence but it must also be demonstrated that its long-range effect is to reduce the total quantity of violence within society."[19]

The article cites the evidence then available that the death penalty is not a deterrent to murder, and that, in fact, the death penalty states tended to be the most violent. The author adds a quote:

" 'Official killing by the state makes killing respectable. It not merely dulls the sensibilities of people to cruelty and inhumanity but actually stimulates cruelty.' "[20]

Professor Reichert objects to the separation in the public mind of the death penalty as being unrelated to the system of values we as society have created for ourselves. He expresses the belief that the criminal law is not complete in itself, but is, rather, an integral part of our total social and political experience. He states:

"When we find that any part of the law fails to reflect the spirit of our moral values, which is the most precious thing we as a society possess, we must do all that we can to correct the deficiency."[21]

Professor William Reichert concludes this remarkable article with this wish:

18. See the discussion at the commencement of this Chapter.
19. Reichert, page 398, 399.
20. Ibid. page 402, citing Henry Weihofen, from "The Urge to Punish."
21. Ibid. page 399.

70

"Let us hope that Kentucky is not the last state to give up the death penalty as it was the last to abandon the practice of public executions."[22]

The arguments made by the professor are still the basis of the abolition movement today, and as we carry on the professor's work we hope we can express the cause for abolition nearly as well as he did.

Kelly Moss was executed on March 2, 1962, adding his name to the list of 162 men electrocuted by the state since electrocutions began in 1911. By an unusual string of circumstances, Moss was the last person executed in Kentucky for 35 years, until July 1, 1997. The initial reason for the long moratorium was the election in 1962 of Governor Edward T. "Ned" Breathitt of Hopkinsville. Governor Breathitt was the first Kentucky governor to publicly oppose the death penalty. He personally believed it was neither right nor effective, and he wanted it abolished.

As fate would have it, the first order on Governor Breathitt's desk following his inauguration was an order for the execution of an inmate on death row whose appeals had come to an end. Governor Breathitt agonized over this for days because he did not want to sign the order, but it was the law. His final decision was he had to do his duty, and he signed the order.

Not long after this news of the pending execution was released, into the Governor's office came the Circuit Court Judge who had presided at the condemned man's trial, and the Commonwealth Attorney who had prosecuted the case. They pleaded with him to do something because they were convinced the man to be executed was not guilty. Governor Breathitt was relieved of his burden, and by agreement the execution order was revoked and the man's sentence was commuted to time served.[23]

22. Ibid. page 417.
23. Interview with former Governor Edward T. Breathitt by the author on Feb. 13, 1999, by telephone.

The Governor's opinion against the death penalty being thus reinforced, he supported legislation in 1964 and 1966 for the abolition of the death penalty, and issued a general stay of all executions during his term of office.[24] The Kentucky General Assembly passed none of the abolition legislation, but it did in the course of its deliberations authorize a study of capital punishment by the Kentucky Legislative Research Commission. The commission's results were published in 1965.[25]

The 17-page factual report by the Legislative Research Commission reads much like the material presented in the subsequent chapters of this book. The report states on page 5: "There is a definite trend throughout the United States toward repealing capital punishment by complete abolition, or disuse. Complete abolition is usually followed by substituting life imprisonment, or a term of years imprisonment."

The Legislative Research Commission Report in Chapter 3 compares the crime rate in states retaining the death penalty and those which have abolished it, and finds, at page 6: "Abolitionist states in the same geographic area as retentionist states do not show a higher capital crime rate. In some cases abolitionist states have a lower capital crime rate than many states that still use capital punishment ... The information available at present clearly shows that no statistical difference exists between states that use the death penalty, and those that have abolished the penalty."[26]

The study lists the arguments generally made by proponents and opponents of the death penalty, and then states the conclusions of the study.

"The statistical information presently available does not

24. *Public Papers of Governor Edward T. Breathitt 1963-1967*, Kenneth E. Harrell, Editor (University Press of Kentucky, Lexington, 1984) page 471.
25. *Capital Punishment*, Informational Bulletin No. 40, 1965, Commonwealth of Kentucky Legislative Research Commission, Frankfort, Ky., hereinafter referred to as Bulletin No. 40.
26. More recent statistics reported in Chapter 3 later in this book show that states retaining the death penalty tend to have more violent crimes than states without the death penalty. Authorities on crime now call this the "brutalizing effect" of the death penalty.

indicate a significant difference in the homicide rates between abolition states and capital punishment states. Further research in this area, conducted over a period of time, will be necessary before any definite conclusions can be obtained. However, most of the evidence available tends to support the abolitionist position, and to disprove the retentionist argument.

"From the material available at present it is clear that the value of the death penalty as a deterrent to the incidence of capital crime is certainly very limited, if not entirely negligible. Social, cultural, and economic conditions seem to have a more important affect on the homicide rate than; capital punishment."[27]

Chapter 3 of this book provides the reader with the further statistical data gathered over the intervening years, that makes the conclusions set forth by the Legislative Research Commission in 1965 to be very definitely correct, indeed.

Governor Breathitt was followed in office in 1968 by a Republican governor, Louie Nunn. Governor Nunn was not for abolishing the death penalty, and in a recent interview he stated, "I was concerned for the safety of the people in the prisons. Without the death penalty, I didn't think they would be safe from the other prisoners." During Governor Nunn's term only one man on death row came up for execution, and the former Governor states, "all the information that I got was that the man was insane, so I didn't sign the death warrant, and he wasn't executed."[28]

Thus, the moratorium on executions in Kentucky continued for another four years. Then, in 1972, the Supreme Court of the United States granted appeals to consolidated death cases from Georgia and Texas, the lead case styled *Furman v. Georgia.* [29] The sole question in these cases was, "Does the imposition and carrying out of the death penalty (in these cases) constitute cruel and unusual punishment in violation

27. Bulletin No. 40, page 10,11.
28. Interview with Gov. Louie Nunn by the author, on Feb. 8, 1999, by telephone.
29. 409 U.S. 15, 92 S.Ct. 2726 (1972).

of the 8th and 14th Amendments to the Constitution?" In a five to four decision the court answered, "Yes." The effect of this decision was to invalidate pending death sentences throughout the country, and accordingly the moratorium in Kentucky was continued indefinitely.

In *Furman v. Georgia*, each of the five Justices in the majority, Justices Douglas, Brennan, Stewart, White, and Marshall, wrote separate opinions, as did each of the four justices in the minority, Justices Blackmun, Powell, Rehnquist, and Chief Justice Burger.

Reading the opinions, I find it difficult to determine accurately the degree to which the individual justices found that the death penalty, under current standards, violates the provisions of the 8th Amendment, prohibiting cruel and unusual punishments. The same history and precedents were discussed by each of our highest Jurists, and the results were confusing at best.

There is little doubt, however, that in 1972 the decision by a state attorney to seek or not seek the death penalty in a specific case rested on wildly varying factors, as did the decision of a jury to sentence or not sentence a defendant to death, or the decision by a judge or a governor to be tough or lenient in a specific case. The only common characteristics among death penalty cases were that a highly disproportionate number of those selected to be executed were poor, of low intelligence, black and accused of a crime against a white. Addiction to alcohol or drugs was endemic.

The attorneys, jurors, judges, and governors authorized by the various state death penalty statutes to operate the death penalty systems carried out their duties with little guidance or oversight, and produced results that were described by one Justice as wanton and freakish, and were clearly troubling, to one degree or another, to all the justices.

After the decision in *Furman v. Georgia* was rendered in 1972, the authorities in Georgia and elsewhere amended their death penalty statutes to limit the discretion previously allowed, and added review mechanisms in an attempt to reduce inequities. Under the new statutes, a new capital conviction was obtained and appealed, and a second case, *Gregg v. Georgia*[30] went to the Supreme Court on the question once again of the constitutionality of the death penalty.

In Kentucky, however, the legislature paid little heed to the Furman decision, and in 1974 amended the statutes to make the death penalty mandatory under certain circumstances. Convictions under this statute when appealed to the Kentucky Court of Appeals were reversed, the court holding the mandatory statute to be unconstitutional.[31]

After arguments were heard in the Supreme Court in *Gregg v. Georgia*, Justices Stewart and White were satisfied with the statutory changes made by Georgia and switched sides, joining Justices Rehnquist, Blackmun, Chief Justice Burger, and new Justice Stevens. The death sentence was now held constitutional.

Following the *Gregg* decision, the Kentucky Legislature met in December 1976, and amended the Kentucky death penalty statute to conform to the Georgia statute, and thereby comply with the *Gregg v. Georgia* decision in the United States Supreme Court.[32]

The new death penalty statute defined the requirements for a capital punishment charge more strictly and established multiple judicial reviews, as was now required. Gradually, over the years there were new convictions and the number of inmates on death row began to increase once again. But the new procedural requirements and the extensive judicial reviews meant ever-lengthening stays on death row.

30. 428 U.S. 153, 96 S.Ct. 2909 (1976). There were additional death penalty cases the Supreme Court heard and decided at the same time, upholding Florida's revised death penalty statute, *Profitt v. Florida*, 428 U.S. 242, 96 S.Ct. 2960 (1976) and upholding the Texas statute, Jurek v. Texas, 428 U.S. 262, 96 S.Ct. 2950 (1976).
31. See: *Boyd v. Commonwealth*, Ky., 550 S.W. 2d 507 (1977); *Self v. Commonwealth*, Ky., 550 S.W. 2d 509 (1977); and *Meadows v. Commonwealth*, Ky., 550 S.W. 511 (1977).
32. Kentucky Acts 1976, Extra Session, Chapter 15, Sections 2 and 3.

In 1985, the Kentucky Legislative Research Commission updated its reports on capital punishment and outlined the new requirements and procedures of the Kentucky death penalty laws. In its review of the continuing debate on the merits of the death penalty the Legislative Research Commission notes, in regard to the increasing expense of the death penalty cases:

"It has long been commonly believed that housing a convicted felon for life is far more expensive than execution. However, some studies are showing that the lengthy appeal process in capital cases makes the death penalty much more expensive.

"Moreover, the amount of time and energy that is expended on capital punishment cases is overwhelming. Kevin McNally, Death Penalty Coordinator for the Department of Public Advocacy in Frankfort, reports that his office is deluged by death penalty cases and must spend the majority of its time working on them. This imbalance means that there is little time to devote to problems of juveniles, the disabled, and the retarded. Mr. McNally explains that the death penalty is a burden to our criminal justice system, 'sucking up huge amounts of criminal justice resources with no payback.' He feels that the time, energy and money expended on capital punishment could be utilized in far more productive areas."

Commenting on the possibility of mistakes being made by the courts in death penalty cases, the report concludes:

"In 1975, just one year before capital punishment was again a reality, two cases were heard that proved that six innocent people had been wrongly condemned. Had the year been 1977, these people may have been executed for murders they did not commit."[33]

The movement in Kentucky to abolish the death penalty continued to grow, even after the *Gregg* decision. Much of the effort was directed toward removing the flaws in the exist-

33. *Capital Punishment*, Research Report No. 218, Legislative Research Commission, Frankfort, Ky., Oct. 1985, pages 13-14.

ing system, until the day would come when there was enough support in Kentucky to accomplish abolition.

In 1990, opponents of the death penalty and others wanting reform sought to persuade the legislature to amend the death penalty statute to prohibit the state from executing the mentally retarded. This was accomplished.[34]

By 1997, one member of death row, Harold McQueen, had exhausted his last appeal, and on July 1, 1997 he was electrocuted at Eddyville State Penitentiary. The execution engendered wide publicity and discussion, and one result was that the ranks of the abolitionists in Kentucky grew.

In 1998, a coalition of opponents of the death penalty successfully lobbied the legislature to enact a Racial Justice Act,[35] which for the first time permits a defendant to present statistical or other evidence of racial prejudice to the court for consideration in a challenge to the death penalty. Kentucky, in this instance, became a national leader as the first state to enact a Racial Justice Act, affecting the death penalty.

Due in part to the wide publicity of the McQueen's execution in 1997, and the publicly expressed objections of many to the visible trauma of death by electrocution, the Kentucky Legislature in 1998 amended the death penalty statute to substitute lethal injections of poisonous substances for executing prisoners, replacing electrocutions. Responding to the objections of physicians and the ethical restraints on the medical profession, subsection (3) of the new statute provides:

"No physician shall be involved in the conduct of an execution except to certify cause of death provided that the condemned is declared dead by another person."

This is the status of the law at the time of this writing. While a majority of the United States Supreme Court Justices may be satisfied that the current statutes provide fair and equitable procedures, the most common characteristics of those condemned to die still are those who are poor, of low intelli-

34. Kentucky Revised Statutes 532.050.
35. Kentucky Revised Statutes 532.300.

gence, black and who have committed crimes against whites and who have addictions to drugs and alcohol.[36]

At the very beginnings of our state, as I noted earlier, our newly elected legislature's first laws on crime and punishment repealed the harsh English and Virginia laws, and abolished capital punishment for all crimes, except murder in the first degree.

In the preamble to that first act, the legislature stated, "the reformation of offenders (is) an object highly meriting the attention of the laws," and "capital punishments, which exterminate instead of reforming, should be the last melancholy resource."

The legislature also limited executions to only those criminals, "whose existence is become inconsistent with the safety of their fellow citizens." Remember, these were the days when there were few jails where dangerous criminals could be safely kept from society. [37]

In 1998, Governor Paul Patton proposed, and the legislature passed, an act providing an additional punishment in capital cases, of imprisonment for life without benefit of probation or parole.[38] This remedy is now available in capital cases, and therefore no individual's existence can any longer be "inconsistent with the safety of their fellow citizens." Where it is necessary and proper, a dangerous individual can be removed from society for the rest of his life,[39] and the danger will never again be present. We no longer need executions to fulfill the mandate of our founding legislature.

36. See, Chapter IV, "Death Row."
37. The Kentucky Legislature did establish a penitentiary in 1798 along with the first criminal justice act, but for many years the penitentiary was more of a problem than a solution. See: R. Crawford, *A History of the Kentucky Penitentiary System 1865-1937*, Dissertation, Graduate School, University of Kentucky, 1955.
38. Kentucky Revised Statute 532.030.
39. I consistently will use the male gender in referring to individuals facing the death penalty for the capital crime of murder, because the 200 people we have executed in this century have all been men. The last female executed in Kentucky was a 13-year-old black girl, hanged in Newcastle in 1865. (See testimony in *Commonwealth vs. Haight*, Indictment No. 85-CR-032, TE Vol. 2, p. 221).

We are coming full circle. Our first legislators, in the enactment of our first criminal code, expressed their belief in the ideas of the enlightenment, that man was capable of improvement and that barbaric punishments should end. Two hundred years later, after enough violence to test the patience of the kindest of 18th century philosophers, we are ready to fulfill our founder's beliefs. We are headed toward abolition, to a society of increasing peace, compassion and fairness.

Our concerns for safety are genuine, and they can be met. It is time now to move on.

CHAPTER III
RATIONALITY

"Violence is necessary, it's as American as cherry pie."
Hubert "Rap" Brown, 1966

Introduction

When we as a community take a historical view of capital punishment it is clear we have been killing in response to wrongs committed either against us as individuals, families, or society, for at least as long as we have been keeping accounts. The response began as an act of survival. Our individual instinct for revenge and society's instinct for retribution, is deeply rooted. It was for tens of thousands of years the way we acted, the way we were conditioned to act, without question.

It is only in the last several hundred years, with the dawn of the age of reason, that any rationality has been focused on capital punishment. Once we began to think about capital punishment in the early eighteenth century the abolition movement began,[1] and not long thereafter our country began. Justice Brennan of the United States Supreme Court writes:

"From the beginning of our nation, the punishment of death has stirred acute public controversy. Although pragmatic arguments for and against the punishment have been frequently advanced, this long-standing and heated controversy cannot be explained solely as the result of differences over the practical wisdom of a particular government policy. At bot-

---

1. Several sources on the history of the death penalty debate are: Archer and Gartner, *Violence & Crime in Cross- National Perspective* (Yale University Press, New Haven, 1982), hereinafter Archer and Gartner; W.M.Green, *Capital Punishment* (Harper and Row, New York, 1967).

tom, the battle has been waged on moral grounds. The country has debated whether a society for which the dignity of the individual is the supreme value can, without a fundamental inconsistency, follow the practice of deliberately putting some of its members to death. In the United States, as in other nations of the western world, 'the struggle about this punishment has been one between ancient and deeply rooted beliefs in retribution, atonement or vengeance on the one hand, and, on the other, beliefs in the personal value and dignity of the common man that were born of the democratic movement of the eighteenth century, as well as beliefs in the scientific approach to an understanding of the motive forces of human conduct, which are the result of the growth of the sciences of behavior during the nineteenth and twentieth centuries.'[2] It is this essentially moral conflict that forms the backdrop for the past changes in and the present operation of our system of imposing death as a punishment for crime."[3]

It is this essentially moral conflict in which we are here engaged, and as we review the arguments raised in the debate we find there is no single factor consistently relied on by the proponents of capital punishment. Their justifications have varied, depending on the conditions and politics of the times. There are, however, five theories in defense of capital punishment that are used most frequently by proponents, which we will discuss, and since all executions have been for murder since the Furman decision in 1972, we will focus the discussion on that crime. The five theories are:

1. Executions will deter murder by others in the future.
2. Society's sense of justice demands executions.
3. Victims' families loss and grief requires executions for justice and closure.
4. It is a waste of taxpayers' money to keep a murderer locked

2. Quoting from T. Sellin, "The Death Penalty, A Report for the Model Penal Code Project of the American Law Institute" 15 (1959).
3. *Furman v. Georgia*, 408 U.S. 296, 92 S.Ct. 2726, 2755 (1972).

up for life with free room and board.

5. Rehabilitation of a murderer is unlikely or impossible.

We will examine each of these theories in light of our situation in Kentucky today. Considering our state's history and experience, and looking at our plans and hopes for Kentucky's future, we will explore just how rational these theories are now.

DETERRENCE

"It is because we highly value human life that we favor the death penalty." [4]

The deterrence advocates argue that the execution of a murderer will save the life of a future victim of a potential murderer – that is, take a life to save a life. This theory logically assumes that the potential murderer is a rational actor weighing the severity of the punishment and the likelihood of his being caught.

But is it so? Does the execution of a murderer cause other potential killers to forego violent behavior?

A prominent Kentucky professor of police studies, Dr. Gary Potter, has written:

"The death penalty, if it is to deter, must be a conscious part of a cost-benefit equation in the perpetrator's mind. There are very few murders that involve that level of rationality or consciousness of the outcomes. Most murders are (1) committed under the influence of drugs or alcohol; (2) committed by people with severe personality disorders; (3) committed during periods of extreme rage or anger; or (4) committed as a result of intense fear. None of these states of mind lends itself

4. Rep. Thomas Kerr in the Kentucky Legislature, Jan. 14, 1998, as quoted in *The Courier-Journal*, Jan. 15, 1998.

to the calm reflection required for a deterrent effect."[5]

The question has been the subject of innumerable statistical research studies nationally, and in Kentucky. It would seem a simple matter. If capital punishment is a deterrent, its adoption by a state should decrease the number of murders; and, if it is a deterrent, the abolition of capital punishment by a state should increase the number of murders.

From all of the research done — by individuals on every side of the question — the results overwhelmingly show that a positive correlation does not exist between the death penalty and a decrease in violence. In fact, contrary results appear more often; executions have a brutalizing effect, rather than act as a deterrent.

Let's look at the record in Kentucky. As a state, we were regularly executing murderers until March 2, 1962, the last execution before the Supreme Court held the death penalty unconstitutional in *Furman v. Georgia*.[6] The Supreme Court in 1976 reversed *Furman*, in *Gregg v. Georgia*,[7] and the next execution was on July 1, 1997.[8] There was a period of 35 years without any executions in this state. What effect did this absence of the death penalty have on the murder rate in Kentucky?

Statistics gathered by the Kentucky State Police, and published annually in their *Crimes in Kentucky Report*, show the history of reported murders from 1970 to 1996, covering the period when we had no executions in Kentucky. The results selected for every ten years after the last execution, and for the most recent year, present this statistical summary:

5. Potter, Gary, "Crime Control and the Death Penalty," *The Advocate Journal of Criminal Justice, Education & Research*, Vol. 19, No. 6, November, 1997, page 37.
6. 409 U.S. 15, 92 S.Ct 2726 (1972).
7. 428 U.S. 153, 96 S.Ct 2909 (1976).
8. The reasons for this long moratorium on executions are presented in Chapter II, "History of the Laws of Capital Punishment in Kentucky."

OFFENSE	YEAR	NUMBER OF MURDERS	RATE PER 100,000
MURDER	1970	335	10.4
MURDER	1980	321	8.8
MURDER	1990	261	7.0
MURDER[9]	1996	227	5.8

These statistics show that during the period when there were no executions in Kentucky, from 1963 to 1997, the murder rate went from 335 per year to 227 per year, a decrease of 30 percent. This is a very significant improvement in our murder rates. This is the one period in our history when there were no executions for the crime of murder, and thus no deterrent, and the murder rates went down. If executions were truly a deterrent, it is reasonable to expect that it would be reflected in some manner in the statistics during this time, and it was not.[10]

The search for evidence of the deterrent effect of capital punishment goes back to the early 19th century when a Massachusetts state Legislator named Robert Rantoul, Jr. developed a sophisticated method of assembling and interpreting data on the death penalty.[11] Rantoul examined long term trends in European countries and found the countries with the fewest executions experienced a decline in the homicide rate - exactly the reverse of what the deterrent theory would predict. When he turned his attention to short term patterns he found that periods with unusually high numbers of executions were followed by increases in the incidence of homicides — again the opposite of what the deterrent theory would anticipate.

9. The rates per 100,000 for the years 1990 and 1996 are not official, but are estimates made with the assistance of the statistical supervisor of the Kentucky State Police.
10. Looking at the results for other violent crimes during the same years shows many increases, so the drop in the murder rate was the exception rather then the rule.
11. Archer and Gartner, *Violence & Crime in Cross-National Perspective* (Yale University Press, New Haven, 1982), page 124.

Many studies followed, and over a period of 50 years there were reports published from Bye (1919), Sutherland (1925), Vold (1932, 1952), Dann (1935), Schuessler (1952), Sellin (1961,1967), and Reckless (1969). T. Sellin reviewed these works and summed them up in his 1967 book, stating: "the presence of the death penalty — in law or practice — does not influence homicide death rates."[12]

Death penalty advocates were unhappy with these findings, and in 1975 a researcher named Ehrlich came up with a different result which advocates gave wide publicity. His findings, using his own formula applied to aggregate homicide data for the entire United States for the period 1933 to 1970, showed a "probability of execution" did reduce homicides.[13]

Because this study was the only one obtaining these results it was widely examined, and attempts to duplicate it using Ehrlich's formula and his economic analysis failed to produce the same results.[14] Many specialists in the field reviewed Ehrlich's work, particularly Bowers and Pierce (1975), Passall and Taylor (1976), Klein, Forst, and Filatov (1978), Loftin (1980), and Brier and Fienberg (1980), and the composite opinion was critical and disagreed with Ehrlich's reported findings.[15]

One of the frequently recurring results of many of these studies is what one author labeled, "the brutalizing effect" of the death penalty. In Rantoul's original studies, cited above, he found an increase in homicides following an execution, and more recent investigators have discovered the same thing. A study by Bowerd and Pierce (1980) examined monthly homicide rates in New York state between 1907 and 1963 and found an average increase of two homicides in the month after an execution. From these and similar studies is born the "anti-deterrent" theory.

12. T. Sellin, ed. *Capital Punishment* (Harper and Row, New York), 1967.
13. I. Ehrlich, "The Deterrent Effect of Capital Punishment," *American Economic Review* 65: 397-417.
14. Archer and Gartner, page 125.
15. Ibid, page 125.

Dr. Potter writes that capital punishment has become a hindrance rather than help in society's fight against violence. He states:

"In fact, the death penalty produces serious crime problems and social problems of its own. Probably most important of these is the fact that death penalty not only doesn't deter murder, it encourages people to kill.

"Studies of capital punishment have consistently shown that homicide actually increases in the time period surrounding an execution. Social scientists refer to this as the 'brutalization effect.' Executions stimulate homicides in three ways: (1) executions desensitize the public to the immorality of killing, increasing the probability that some people will then decide to kill; (2) the state legitimizes the notion that vengeance for past misdeeds is acceptable; and (3) executions also have an imitative effect, where people actually follow the example set by the state, after all, people feel if the government can kill its enemies, so can they.

" ... While not a direct test of the brutalization effect it is, nonetheless, instructive to note that in post-*Furman* period marking the reintroduction of capital punishment ... about one-third of all executions in the United States have occurred in Georgia and Louisiana, and in both states the murder rate has increased markedly ... ."[16]

Proponents of the deterrent theory respond to the negative results of almost all these studies by asking for more studies, or suggesting that the right questions are not being asked.

An extensive study in 1978 by William C. Burley in North Carolina resulted in this summary and conclusion:

" ... we have examined the deterrence hypothesis of a significant inverse relationship between the certainty of execution and homicide rates for the

16. Gary Potter, "Crime Control and the Death Penalty," *The Advocate Journal of Criminal Justice, Education & Research*, Vol. No. 6, November, 1997, page 39, 40.

state of North Carolina for the period 1910 to 1962. Three models of the execution rate - homicide rate relationship were considered, with two measures of offense rates being examined ... .

" ... For each of the execution rate-homicide rate models, for the two measures of homicide, and for both the linear and nonlinear models, analysis resulted in a very consistent pattern of findings. Contrary to the deterrence hypothesis, throughout the analysis certainty of execution was not found to be significantly inversely related to homicide rates ... That is, for the years considered (1910-1962) changes in the certainty of execution and homicide rates were found to be generally unrelated factors.

" ... For the period examined here, levels of unemployment would appear to have had a significant effect on levels of homicide, and levels of executions would appear to have been unrelated to homicide rates. If we assume that the observed relationship between these two factors and homicide holds equally well today, (and history probably provides us with the best means of guidance here), then there would appear to be little to no hope that the use of the death penalty can provide an effective means of deterring murder. Rather, measures aimed at improving socioeconomic conditions and other negative consequences of unemployment would appear to hold much more promise in dealing with this dimension of the crime problem in North Carolina."[17]

In Kentucky there is not, as we have seen, any evidence that capital punishment has been a deterrent to murder. The evidence points to quite the contrary. What do we find when we look specifically at the other states?

17. Archer and Gartner, page 125.

There are 12 states that do not have capital punishment. They are Alaska, Hawaii, Iowa, Maine, Massachusetts, Michigan, Minnesota, North Dakota, Rhode Island, Vermont, West Virginia and Wisconsin. There are 10 additional states that have capital punishment statutes but for a number of reasons have not had an execution for a long time. So it is the remaining 28 states, Kentucky included, that are actively proceeding with state executions. How do they compare in murder rates with the non-death penalty states?

The average murder rate per 100,000 people in states with capital punishment in 1996 was 7.1; in non-death penalty states it was 3.6. Even when the states are neighbors the contrast is striking; death penalty Missouri — eight per 100,000, and neighbor, non-death penalty Iowa – two per 100,000; death penalty Virginia — 7.7 per 100,000, non-death penalty West Virginia — 3.9 per 100,000.

From 1976 (*Gregg v. Georgia*) through May 1998 there have been 461 executions in the United States, and the vast majority (81%) were in the South: Texas 152, Virginia 50, Florida 43, Louisiana 24, Georgia 22, Alabama 17, and South Carolina 13. The murder rate in the South during this time was the highest in the country, averaging nine per 100,000 people, while in the Northeast, where less than one percent of the executions took place, the average rate was 5.4 per 100,000 people.[18] While many factors can affect these rates, there is no way they can be cited to support the deterrent theory. In fact, they all point in the other direction.

We will turn now to Europe and England. It was once said, "There is no country on the face of the earth in which there are so many offenses according to law punishable by death as in England,"[19] and the struggle for abolition was a very long one. But on November 8, 1965, Queen Elizabeth II signed the

18. These statistics are gathered and published by Death Penalty Information Center, 1320 Eighteenth Street NW, Washington, D.C.
19. Sir Samuel Romilly. See: Eugene B.Block, *When Men Play God*, (Cragmont Publications, San Francisco, 1983), page 146.

"Murder Bill," which abolished capital punishment in England for a trial period of five years. Well before the end of that time Parliament made abolition permanent. The British until recently had an exception for piracy and treason during wartime, but that now has been removed and Britain has, in fact, had no executions since 1965.

In France, the abolition movement of "la peine de mort" dates back to the 18th century and Robespierre. The guillotine was brought in to use in the French Revolution after its inventor, Dr. Joseph Guillotine, promised, "With my machine, I can take off your head in a wink, and you won't feel anything." [20]

The French made much use of Dr. Guillotine's invention, but opposition to the death penalty continued, and after World War II a major movement led by novelist Albert Camus ultimately brought abolition.

During the campaign, Camus wrote:

"It is a strange law that recognizes the murder it commits and remains forever ignorant of the crime it prevents. But what will remain of this power of example if it is proved that the death penalty has another power, this one quite real, which commits men to the worst excesses of shame, madness and murder."

In September 1981, the French National Assembly by a vote of 363 to 117 abolished capital punishment in France and President Francois Mitterand signed the Proclamation.[21]

Now there are no countries in Western Europe with the death penalty, and the rate of murders per 100,000 people is significantly lower than it is in the United States.

As we look back over the studies and reported experience, we find there is no evidence that capital punishment is a deterrent in Kentucky. In the rest of the states, with and without capital punishment, there is no evidence that capital punishment is a deterrent. In England and Western Europe, where

20. Ibid. page 177.
21. Ibid. page 182.

there no longer is capital punishment, there is no evidence it was ever a deterrent.

It is not enough to say, or to feel, that the death penalty is bound to be a deterrent. Without evidence, we are put in a position of using a false theory to justify some other unspoken motive or goal. To justify an execution, the killing must really be a deterrent; there must be real lives that are saved, and we must be able to know that.

In Thucydides' accounts of the Athenian wars, he relates a debate about whether the citizens of Mytelene should be killed in retribution for their revolt against Athenian rule. Mytelene had long been an ally of Athens, but in 428 it rescinded its treaty and formed an alliance with the Spartans. Athens responded by invading Mytelene, capturing the city, and the Athenian Assembly decreed punishment by death to the men and enslavement for the women and children. Citizens of Athens raised objections, and Thucydides records that Cleon spoke for the punishment, and Diodotus spoke against, citing a very negative critique of the deterrent effect of capital punishment. In the debate he said, "If we must act in accordance with our interests (and kill the citizens of Mytelene), driven by our fears of one another, then talk about justice cannot possibly be anything more than talk."[22] This argument prevailed.

In Kentucky, if we continue capital punishment driven by our fears of one another, with deterrence as our excuse, justice cannot possibly be anything more than talk. We will be no better than our ancient savage ancestors, or, more recently, our Hatfields and McCoys, taking revenge upon revenge.

Deterrence is not a viable theory, nor a valid justification for the death penalty.

22. Michael Walzer, *Just And Unjust Wars*, (Basic Books, Inc., New York, 1977) cited at page 10.

JUSTICE FOR SOCIETY

*"In the end I believe the death penalty, ironically, is
not just a lust for revenge but a desperate expression
of a longing for a safer world, a world free of fear."*
Mario Cuomo

There is a passion in each of us for a just society.

The role of punishment in a just society has been the
subject of thought and discussion for thousands of years. That
discussion intensifies with the ultimate punishment, the death
penalty.

In thinking about the role of capital punishment in
society, we resist admitting to vengeful feelings, and we shy
away from "God's will." Most often we use the word retribution.

The first definition given in Webster's for retribution
(from the Latin retribuerer - to pay back) is "recompense or
reward." The second is "the dispensing or receiving of reward
or punishment; esp. in the hereafter." And the third is "something given or exacted in recompense; esp. punishment."[23]

The definitions incorporate both religion and revenge,
and these are the elements most prominent in the death penalty debate.

In response to a murder, we feel an urge that the killer
get what he gave–death. This is retribution. Yet what is the
basis of this desire for retribution, and does retribution lead
to a more just society in Kentucky?

We will examine the sources of our concepts of retribution from the viewpoint of those who support the death
penalty and the views of the abolitionists. There is, as I've
noted, a mingling of revenge and religion in these feelings,
and in some examples they become one and the same.

We look no further than Genesis 9:6, in the story of Noah:

23. Webster, *New Collegiate Dictionary*, 1981.

"whoso sheddeth man's blood,
by man shall his blood be shed"[24]

Scholars of the Old Testament interpret God's edict not as a moral demand, nor as intimidation, but as ritual. Human life and blood are sacred; whoever sheds it forfeits his own. "The death which sanctions death is ceremonial, celebrative, ritual."[25]

The blood and life of each belongs to God — so it is forbidden to eat blood, and to kill a human; if you do, you will be killed. It is not a moral matter — a second wrong does not make a right. It is not a civil matter — it is not a deterrent and it started before government. It is a sacrifice to God. "The killing of a killer is not a civil, non religious matter. It is a sacrificial act."[26]

Lloyd Bailey in *Capital Punishment: What the Bible Says*, gives his interpretation:

"Life originated by a special act of the Deity (by the power of the divine breath, as the ancient story in Gen. 2:7 put it). Consequently, humans were not free to terminate it, save under conditions specified by God. Even food animals must be brought to the sanctuary and slaughtered in a pre-scribed ritual whereby the blood is removed. Failure to do so results in 'bloodguilt' (Lev. 17:4), a term which is elsewhere used for the murder of a human being (Exod. 22:2). How much more the offense, therefore, if human life ('created in the im-age of God,' Gen. 1:26) is taken without proper sanction! One has acted arrogantly against a life force that is an extension of Gods own life-giving power. It is, to put it boldly, 'an attack upon God.' Even an animal that kills a human is to be de-stroyed (Exod. 21:28). A human who does so all the more for-

24. The biblical quotes in the text are from the King James' version of the Bible.
25. John Howard Yoder, *Noah's Covenant, the New Testament, and Christian Social Order*, in Hugo Adam Bedau's *Death Penalty in America* (Oxford University Press, New York, 1997), hereinafter Yoder, page 435.
26. Ibid. page 435.

feits any right to life (Gen. 9:1-7)."[27]

So initially, we find a concept of sacrificial ritual; a dogmatic obeisance to God, without thought to punishment or deterrence.

When Moses descended from Mount Sinai, he gave Israel the Ten Commandments to guide their lives as God's covenant people. One of them was, "Thou shalt not kill"(Exod. 20:13). Yet, throughout the Old Testament the death penalty is commanded for many offenses.

The rationale to this conundrum, as I understand it, is a belief that God has established two separate arenas of moral activity —private morality and public morality. The inconsistency is resolved under this view by separating how a person acts individually, and how he or she acts as an agent of government.

In this view, God recognizes governments, and the Noachian and Mosaic Covenants commanding killing apply to these governments, while the prohibition, *Thou shalt not kill*, applies only to individuals acting on their own. Of course, during most of our history it has been believed that our rulers were divinely selected and would therefore be particularly qualified to carry out God's vengeance. God told Israel to engage in total warfare against the Canaanite tribes, and Israel's leaders did as God commanded.

It is said in Deuteronomy 21:18-21:

> "If a man have a stubborn and rebellious son that will not obey the voice of his father, or the voice of his mother, and though they chasten him, will not hearken unto them, then shall his father and mother lay hold on him and bring him out unto the elders of his city and unto the gate of his place; and they shall say unto the elders of his city, 'This our son is stubborn and rebellious, he will

27. Ibid. page 427.

not obey our voice; he is a glutton and a drunk-
ard.' And all the men of his city shall stone him to
death with stones; so shalt thou put away the evil
from the midst of thee; and all Israel shall hear,
and fear."

The parents, should they wish, could not kill their son.
That would be murder. But they were authorized, even commanded, to testify to the elders, who were then empowered to
purge the evil.

H. Wayne House concludes his treatise *on Moral Arguments for Capital Punishment* with this summary:

"The biblical evidence for capital punishment may be
summarized with these observations. In Genesis 9, God estab-
lishes a covenant with all humanity in which, among other
things, he gives mankind permission to exercise judicial authority among themselves to exercise his wrath against the
crime of murder. The established penalty for this act is death.
The Mosaic Covenant established, among other things, the
rules and regulations by which the descendants of Abraham
would live as those under the Abrahamic Covenant. Those
rules mandated capital punishment for a number of crimes,
including murder. While the laws of the Mosaic Covenant,
including those of capital punishment, are no longer binding
in the New Testament economy, the provisions of the Noachian
Covenant are still in force. This Covenant provides capital
punishment for the crime of murder today. Nothing in the
teachings of Jesus or the apostles contradicts this sanctioning.
Capital punishment is a proper course of action for governments today in the exercise of their divine mandate to punish
evil."

Ernest Van Den Haag, a leading proponent of the
death penalty, has also written widely on the subject. In the
University of California-Davis Law Review he wrote in 1985 on
the morality of the death penalty.

"The Lord is often quoted as saying 'Vengeance is

Mine.' He did not condemn vengeance. He merely reserved it to Himself - and to the government. For in the same epistle He is also quoted as saying that the ruler is 'the minister of God, a revenger, to execute wrath upon him that doeth evil.' The religious notion of hell indicates that the biblical God favored harsh and everlasting punishment for some. However, particularly in a secular society, we cannot wait for the day of judgment to see murderers consigned to hell. Our courts must 'execute wrath upon him that doeth evil' here and now."[28]

There is in the pro-death penalty writings a strong reliance on the many Old Testament references to death as punishment, and a separation of private and public morality to accommodate the Commandment, Thou shalt not kill. From a religious perspective it then follows, as Professor Van Den Haag stresses, that whether the killing is ceremonial expiation, or God's vengeance, it is our public officials administering the death penalty who are now carrying out God's will.

The abolitionists respond, also heavily laden with biblical texts, reminding us that the first murderer, Cain, who had only God as judge and jury, was spared the death penalty. He was marked, and spent the rest of his days as a warning to others of the evil of killing.

And then comes the New Testament, the birth, death and resurrection of Jesus.

John Howard Yoder writes:

"It is the clear testimony of the New Testament, especially of the Epistle to the Hebrews, that the ceremonial requirements of the Old Covenant find their end - both in the sense of fulfillment and in the sense of termination - in the high-priestly sacrifice of Christ. 'Once for all' is the good news. Not only is the sacrifice of bulls and goats, turtledoves

28. Hugo Adam Bedau, *The Death Penalty in America* (Oxford University Press, Oxford, 1997) pages 451-452.

and wheatcakes at an end; the fact that Christ died for our sins, once for all, the righteous one for the godless (Heb. 9:26-28; 1 Pet. 3:18), puts an end to the entire expiatory system, whether it be enforced by priests in Jerusalem or by executioners anywhere else."[29]

Jesus, in the Sermon on the Mount:
"Ye have heard that it was said, Thou shalt love thy neighbor, and hate thine enemy: but I say unto you, Love your enemies, and pray for them that persecute you; that ye may be sons of your father who is in heaven: for he maketh his sun to rise on the evil and the good, and sendeth rain on the just and the unjust (Matt 5:43)."

The proponents of the death penalty respond that nowhere in the New Testament does Christ specifically denounce the death penalty, and that, in fact, Jesus acknowledged Caesar's general authority.

When Jesus was warned by Pilate, "Knowest thou not that I have power to release thee, and have power to crucify thee?" Jesus answers, "Thou wouldest have no power against me, except it were given thee from above; therefore he that delivered me unto thee hath greater sin (John 19:10)." Jesus' response is against his accusers; he does not question the authority of Pilate to order an execution.

Jesus was tested, as told in John 8:3-11:
"And the scribes and the Pharisees bring a woman taken in adultery; and having set her in the midst, they say unto him, Teacher, this woman hath been taken in adultery, in the very act. Now in the law Moses commanded us to stone such: what then sayest thou of her? And this they said trying him that they might have whereof to accuse him. But Jesus stooped down, and with his finger wrote on the ground. But when they continued asking him, he lifted up himself, and said unto

29. Yoder, page 436.

them, He that is without sin among you, let him first cast a stone against her. And again he stooped down, and with his finger wrote on the ground. And they, when they heard it, went out one by one, beginning from the eldest, even unto the last; and Jesus was left alone, and the woman, where she was, in the midst. And Jesus lifted up himself, and said unto her, Woman, where are they? Did no man condemn thee? And she said, No Man, Lord. And Jesus said, Neither do I condemn thee; go thy way; from henceforth sin no more."

The abolitionists contend that Christ did not condone killing either by an individual or by government, and that the message of his life was love and redemption. On the cross, Jesus said, "Father, forgive them; for they know not what they do."[30]

Supporters of the death penalty disagree, as one writer states:

"Throughout his life Jesus obeyed the Mosaic Code and as Messiah to Israel, demanded obedience to its precepts. He refocused its demands upon the attitudes of its adherents, not just their acts. When confronted by hypocritical, false witnesses he exposed them for what they were and extended mercy to the guilty. We conclude, therefore, that Jesus accepted the Mosaic Code, complete with capital punishment, and did nothing, by word or deed, to abrogate the death penalty."[31]

The answer from the scriptures regarding support or abolishment of capital punishment is in the eyes of the beholder. From the violence of the Old Testament to the violence of the New Testament, there are messages of hate and love, vengeance and forgiveness, for the use of advocates on any side of the issue.

The biblical text and the partisan rhetoric notwithstanding, it is certain when looking at our history that the earthly churches, before and after the Reformation, were staunch sup-

30. Luke 23:34.
31. H. Wayne House, *The New Testament and Moral Arguments for Capital Punishment*, in Hugo Adam Bedau's *Death Penalty in America*, page 419.

porters of the death penalty, which was exercised regularly and often to punish both the heretic and the criminal.

James Megivern, a theologian scholar, says:

"The death penalty with its rituals had been more and more thoroughly grounded in religion over the previous five centuries (12th through 16th). Its justification, even glorification, in theological and canonical treatises left even the best informed observer with the understanding that it was an integral part of God's eternal plan. If tempted to waver on this, one needed only to consult the bedrock authorities from Aquinas to Suarez. Questioning it could seem an act of arrogant temerity. If one did not believe in the death penalty, what other parts of the Christian faith might one also be daring or arrogant enough to doubt or deny?"[32]

This, however, was not the experience in the Jewish tradition. While the Hebrew laws and customs recognized the death penalty and the many sanctions of the Old Testament, the stringent requirements of agreement of the many judges called to try a capital case made death penalty imposition a rarity.

In the Christian world it was not until the very late 17th century that questions were raised publicly of the Church's authority, and on the issue of the death penalty, the first major work in opposition was Cesare Beccaria's *On Crime and Punishment* published in 1764. Voltaire hailed the work and the Catholic Church banned it.[33]

The powerful forces of reason that arose in the 18th century, carrying with it a passionate belief in the principles of equality, justice and individual freedom, have for the last 300 years revolutionized our world, and continue to shape the death penalty debate and its eventual outcome here in Kentucky and throughout the South.

32. James J. Megivern, *The Death Penalty, An Historical and Theological Survey* (Paulist Press, New York, 1997), page 212.
33. Ibid. page 215.

But in Kentucky we have, up to this time, resisted the abolition movement of the enlightenment era, and we continue with the death penalty. Having thought about the biblical antecedents, we can reflect on how much we have perpetuated the ceremonial rituals of the middle ages and beyond. Each participant, including the condemned, has a codified role in our current system, reflecting a model from the past.

Once the death sentence is pronounced, a ritualistic debate begins in the Appellate Courts, with nine specific procedural steps. The debate is about a man's life, and the issues are the technicalities of procedures, of form rather than substance. The ending is almost always preordained.

At the conclusion of the ninth step, the warden of the penitentiary (The High Executioner) takes his place, each of his preparations codified as ritual: the selection of the execution team (who remain anonymous; no one knows who pulls the death switch, or unleashes the poison), the separation and preparation of the condemned man, the arrangement for security, and passes for selected witnesses. On the warden's desk next to his chair is the special telephone connecting him to the Supreme Court of Kentucky and the Supreme Court of the United States (The High Priests), and the Governor of the Commonwealth.

The time for the execution is set for just after midnight, the witching hour. A ceremonial last meal is prepared and eaten, prayers are said, and the Warden appears and reads to the condemned man the Order of Execution. A solemn procession to the death chamber begins, accompanied by spirituals sung by the inmates in the cells facing the long hall. The witnesses are ushered into a room with a window view of the death chamber. A curtain is drawn while the condemned man is strapped into the wooden chair and electrodes connected, or lashed to a gurney and needles inserted. The curtain is opened and the condemned man is permitted to speak his last words upon this earth, to cleanse his soul.

The warden sits by the telephone, and the last petition

is denied by the Kentucky Supreme Court, the last petition is denied by the United States Supreme Court, and the last thing that can save the condemned man is a word from on high, the Governor. The warden waits, dispensation does not come, the word is passed, the lever is pulled, or the drugs injected, and the act is completed.

This is high drama ritual. One can only wonder. This ceremony is so reminiscent of the ceremonies of expiation that were such a part of our distant past. What is it that causes us to proceed in such a manner?

Not having an answer, we return to the revolution of enlightenment beginning in the 18th century. It was a long struggle, but on the issue of the death penalty, the enlightenment movement for abolition ultimately gained wide acceptance in Christian churches.

The Pope of the Roman Catholic Church, John Paul II, issued a long Encyclical Letter in 1995, *Evangelium Vitae, on the Value and Inviolability of Human Life*, which in Chapter III, Section 56, entitled "YOU SHALL NOT KILL, God's Holy Law," he speaks directly about capital punishment. The Pontiff does not mention the long history of the death penalty in the Church, nor join the discussion of Old Testament expiation ceremonies, nor the personal views of Jesus, but rather speaks to us of morality in today's society:

"On this matter (of the death penalty) there is a growing tendency, both in the Church and in civil society to demand that it be applied in a very limited way or even that it be abolished completely...

"The primary purpose of the punishment which society inflicts is 'to redress the disorder caused by the offense.'

"It is clear that for these purposes to be achieved, *the nature and extent of the punishment* must be carefully evaluated and decided upon, and ought not to go to the extreme of executing the offender except in cases of absolute necessity; in other words, when it would not be possible otherwise to defend society. Today, however, as a result of steady improvements in the organization of the penal system, such cases are very rare, if not practically non-existent.

"In any event, the principle set forth in the new Catechism of the Catholic Church remains valid."

This Catechism of the Catholic Church reads:

"If bloodless means are sufficient to defend human lives against an aggressor and to protect the public order, and the safety of persons, public authority must limit itself to such means, because they better correspond to the concrete conditions of the common good and are more in conformity to the dignity of the human person."

The Catholic Church in Kentucky is actively opposed to the death penalty. The leader of the Kentucky Coalition to Abolish the Death Penalty is a Catholic priest, and he is joined by many other priests, bishops, and lay leaders throughout the Commonwealth.

The Kentucky Council of Churches and its members actively oppose the death penalty. The list of all the churches whose leadership and congregations have gone on record as opposing the death penalty is long and impressive, and includes:[34] American Baptist Churches in the U.S.A.; American Friends Service Committee; the American Jewish Committee; Christian Church (Disciples of Christ); Church of the Brethren; the Episcopal Church; Evangelical Lutheran Church in America; the General Association of General Baptists; the Mennonite Church; the Moravian Church in America; National Council of the Churches of Christ in the U.S.A.; the Orthodox Church in America; Presbyterian Church (U.S.A.); Reformed Church in America; Reorganized Church of Jesus Christ of Latter Day Saints; Unitarian Universalist Association; United Church of Christ; United Methodist Church; and the United States Catholic Conference.

---

34. For a more complete list, and copies of statements against capital punishment made by each of the organizations, contact, Religious Organizing Against the Death Penalty Project, c/o American Friends Service Committee, 1501 Cherry Street, Philadelphia, PA 19102 (pclark@afsc.org).

Those who believe in capital punishment as a dictate from God now find the vast majority of our religious leaders and religious institutions in deep disagreement. There is no longer church authority for the death penalty.

Retribution by killing no longer has a holy sanction, which leaves it standing solely as revenge, personal, individual and societal revenge, not divine.

Without a religious foundation, and without deterrence as a justification for executions, how then do we go about handling our feelings of anger and fear when we read of a murder? How do we satisfy our need for action, for a response, for justice?

The fact is, after the initial adrenaline rush to vengeance is over, the response of "kill the murderer" is never a satisfactory answer to our needs. Our needs, proven over and over, are that a suspected murderer be promptly and fairly accused, fairly tried, and if found guilty, severely punished. The duty of the state to protect each citizen against unlawful violence by others is a major component of our social compact. If we don't have police, prosecutors, defense lawyers, courts, and a criminal justice system that accomplishes this service, then our agreements have not been kept, and anarchy can result.

But capital punishment does not, and has never, aided this process. The existence of state executions as punishment is a major reason for breakdowns in our criminal justice system and our not achieving swift and just punishment for murderers. Capital punishment, perhaps because of its severity, has never brought out the best in our criminal justice system. We do not do well in selecting who shall be executed, and because of our deep fears of making a mistake, the process takes woefully long.

Each of us needs to have confidence in our system of criminal justice. We need to know that those running the system care about our safety, and that when a murder occurs the authorities will respond so that each of us, as individuals, knows that we do matter, that our collective society cares, and that it will protect us.

This should be our goal, and it is my conviction that capital punishment in Kentucky hinders our accomplishment of this goal.

Justice for society, and indeed society's sense of justice, will be best served by the abolition of the death penalty.

JUSTICE FOR VICTIMS' FAMILIES

> *In this world*
> *Hate never yet dispelled hate.*
> *Only Love dispels hate.*
> *This is the law,*
> *Ancient and inexhaustible.*
>
> Teachings of the Buddha,
> From the *Dhammapada*

We have looked at the utilitarian value of executions as a deterrent, and have found it wanting. We have examined society's role in executions, and now we need to consider the rights and needs of the victim's families. What does an execution accomplish for a victim's family?

Criminal laws punishing wrongdoing are, in theory at least, enacted by legislatures for the good of society generally, rather than responding to the fears of one segment of society over another, or providing personal retribution for the victims and their families. In practice, however, our criminal laws do reflect the fears of those in power, and their views of victim's rights.

For victim's families, a murdered member is a unique loved individual, taken needlessly, criminally. One life is ended, and many others are disastrously affected; spouses, children, parents, siblings and friends alike are devastated.

The interests and rights of the victims' families at this point need very careful and specific attention. There is no deeper rage, anguish, or loss than that numbing surge that comes with the news that someone deeply loved is gone—unexpectedly, without reason or explanation, only with malice.

The victim can no longer speak. Does the victim's family have a right to demand the death penalty? Will execution of the criminal satisfy that rage or ease the grief? Or does that even matter? This, to me, is one of the most important questions in the entire issue of capital punishment. I have not personally experienced that grief, so I cannot possibly know what it is like. I must listen with care and compassion to what those directly affected say.

Grief is individual, and universal. Enormous grief is profound, and one of the most difficult of all emotions to resolve.

In the preparation of this book I have looked in vain for clinical studies on the effect of the execution of the murderer in resolving the grief of the family of the murdered victim. Does another killing help closure? Does it abate the anger?

In a 1993 paper in *Law & Society Review*, Professor Franklin E. Zimring discusses studies of the death penalty in social science literature, and outlines a range of important questions that need to be researched, including what he calls, "Victim's Impact." Dr. Zimring asks:

"What is the effect of capital punishment on the families of homicide victims? The close relations of homicide victims are frequently identified as the intended special beneficiaries of a death penalty. Is this the case? Or does the death penalty delay closure and healing for those close to victims in cases where death penalty trials and sentences take place?"[35]

These are precisely the questions, but to my knowledge no one has yet responded to the call for clinical research in this area.

We must, therefore, look to the empirical evidence at hand, and examine it as carefully and fairly as possible. There

35. *Law & Society Review*, Vol. 27, No. 1. (1993) page 14.

may be as many different answers as there are different individuals engaged in this unfortunate struggle. It is not for me to attempt to judge, but it is necessary and important that we understand the process, to gain insight into the factors that assist the families of homicide victims dissolve the hate and find closure for their grief.

There is, at the outset, a major problem in gathering empirical evidence. Many victims' families are not open to discussion. Whatever their feelings about the murderer and his execution, many will not, or simply cannot, talk about it publicly. But there are a number of exceptions, and there are victims' family organizations with collective experiences that can give us considerable insights.

U. S. News & World Report, June 16, 1997 edition, contains a report entitled, "The Place For Vengeance"[36] in which reporters gather a number of incidents of victims' families speaking out about capital punishment.

The authors first deal with the Texas execution of crack cocaine addict Kenneth Harris for the rape and murder of Lisa Haack. The victim's family attended the execution, and just before he died, Harris said: "I hope you can go on with your lives and we can put an end to this." Putting an end to it is what so many victims' families seek, the authors believe.

The article records some of the statements of the victims, and their families, of the Oklahoma City bombing by Timothy McVeigh.

"Off the witness stand, survivors expressed their belief that killing McVeigh would be just, given their loss, and many vented their fury. 'The sooner (McVeigh) meets his maker, the sooner justice will be served," said Darlene Welch, whose 4-year-old niece, Ashley, was killed in the blast. 'He will get what he deserves in the afterlife, where he will meet Hitler and Jeffrey Dahmer,' says Ernie Ross, who suffered serious injuries

---

36. Article by Shannon Brownlee, Dan McGraw, and Jason Vest, *U.S.News & World Report*, June 16, 1997, Vol. 122, Issue 23, pages 23-32.

from the blast while working across the street. Another survivor suggested that McVeigh should have one leg amputated and then be suspended over sharpened, growing bamboo shoots that would pierce his body."

The authors comment: "The grieving process for a murder victim is somewhat like that for anyone else: disbelief, anger, grief, and then, finally for some, acceptance. But survivors of homicide victims rarely move easily through these stages. Murder often taps a well of rage that can drown out all other emotions."

Richard Estell's seven year-old daughter Ashley, was abducted, raped and killed by sex offender Michael Blair. When he is executed, Estell plans to be there: "For me, it is partly closure and partly the focus on personal revenge. I want to see him gone. Death by lethal injection is too good for Blair. I can't get it out of my mind what my daughter must have felt. I'd really like to see him put in with the general prison population (where he would likely be raped himself). That would be proper punishment."

Linda Kelly of Houston watched the execution of the murderer of her two children: "When I was standing there watching him, this anger came back to me. All I could think of was that he stood there and looked at my precious children and shot them in the head. I kept thinking, I hate you for what you did, I hate you for taking the father of my two grandbabies."

Kelly said the execution left her unsatisfied. "You stand there and you watch a man take two gasps and it's over. I would like to have seen him humiliated a little bit. I think that he should have been brought in and strapped down in front of us. My son dies after being shot in the face and choking on his own blood. We make it too easy (on killers)."

Danny Roberts' brother, David, was a 23 year-old Paris, Texas, police officer shot and killed by a robbery suspect. David left a wife about to give birth to their son. Roberts attended the execution of the killer, Patrick Rogers, and said: "After it was done, we came out, and it was like, 'Is that it?' My brother suffered terribly when he died. I really wanted to see them bring (Patrick Rogers) into the room and strap him down. They should have let us see a little bit of the terror in Roger's face that my brother must have felt."

Oklahoma State Senator Brooks Douglas' parents were murdered; he and his sister–who was raped–were nearly killed by assailants. It took seventeen years for the trials and hearings. Douglass states: "I was criticized for fostering revenge. So what? Who are we to question what a person's feelings are when they go view an execution? There is no other party that has more to benefit from seeing the killer executed than a family member."

Paula Foster's daughter, Jennifer, was killed by David Herman in a Texas nightclub robbery. When the killer was convicted and sentenced to die, Mrs. Foster said: "God, you don't know how much I wanted that." But she expressed anger at the judicial system: "It was always the state of Texas vs. David Lee Herman. You felt like you're not important. (The prosecutors) have no idea of your need to be involved."

One of the most forthright statements favoring executions on behalf of victims' families was written by Jeff Jacoby, columnist for the Boston Globe. Mr. Jacoby states he was upset at the New York Capital Defenders office because their attorneys were reportedly seeking mercy for their clients. The Capital Defenders' mission is defending indigent individuals accused of capital crimes. Mr. Jacoby states, in part:

"There is little enough we can do to ease the pain of grieving survivors, but hanging murderers would help. Many families can find no peace as long as the slayer of their loved one lives. They are filled with rage and despair; they want the killer dead. By seeking the death penalty for willful murderers, society can offer these families a measure of comfort, and assure them that their loss is taken seriously.

"The enemies of capital punishment declare that putting murderers to death achieves nothing but vengeance — mere retribution that dehumanizes society.

"They are wrong. For one thing, executing those who murder achieves a lot. It saves lives. It puts proven killers permanently out of commission. It secures justice.

"Moreover, there is nothing 'mere' about vengeance. The desire for revenge is at the core of every system of criminal law. The desire to hurt those who have hurt others is normal and healthy, a human instinct as natural as recoiling from a snake — and as self protective. Revenge is honorable and moral, so long as it is meted out fairly and lawfully, by a court sitting in justice."[37]

Sister Helen Prejean, a New Orleans nun, came to know and counsel murderers on death row. In carrying out her mission in Louisiana, she wrote about her experiences in *Dead Man Walking*, which became a best seller and was made into a movie starring Susan Sarandon and Sean Penn.

Sister Prejean's focus initially was on death row inmates to whom she became a spiritual adviser. Through her experiences she came to view state executions as horrific and inhuman, and she became a strong abolitionist. Her neglect of the cares and needs of the victims of these murderers was forcefully brought to her attention by a victim's father, and thereafter she worked extensively with victims' families and helped start a victim support group in New Orleans.

Sister Prejean's book provides many insights into the roles of both retribution and forgiveness in the healing process. The couple from whom she learned the most was Vernon and Elizabeth Harvey. Their daughter, Faith, was abducted, raped and stabbed to death by Robert Willie and Joseph Vacaro.

When Sister Prejean first visited the Harveys and listened to their story, she writes, "Hearing the details of Faith's vicious murder, I find myself sucked into the Harveys' rage."[38]

Both Vernon and Elizabeth Harvey were intent on seeing at least one of the killers, Willie, executed for the murder

37. Reprinted in *The Courier-Journal*, Louisville, Ky., Dec. 15, 1996.
38. Helen Prejean, *Dead Man Walking*, (Vintage Books, New York, 1994), page 145.

of their daughter. Sister Prejean was spiritual adviser to Willie.

As the story unfolds, Sister Prejean seeks and finds understanding of the terrible anger and grief of the Harveys, while at the same time she reaches out to Willie to help him find remorse and some redemption. In this remarkable process, Sister Prejean becomes very close, and much needed, by both parties.

The Harveys knew Sister Prejean was an active abolitionist, and they listened to her arguments against the death penalty. She used a Mahatma Ghandi saying, "If everyone took an eye for an eye, the whole world would be blind."

Vernon Harvey was unmoved. His rage and his hurt were too great. Finally at the execution, Willie looked at the Harveys and his final words were: "I would just like to say, Mr. and Mrs. Harvey, that I hope you get some relief from my death. Killing people is wrong. That's why you've put me to death. It makes no difference whether it's citizens, countries, or governments, killing is wrong."

Two years after the execution the Harveys again invited Sister Prejean to visit them, and they talked of Faith's death and Willie's execution. Sister Prejean recounts:

"Vernon begins to cry. He just can't get over Faith's death, he says. It happened six years ago but for him it's like yesterday, and I realize that now, with Robert Willie dead, he doesn't have an object for his rage. He's been deprived of that, too. I know that he could watch Robert Willie killed a thousand times and it could never assuage his grief. He had walked away from the execution chamber with his rage satisfied but his heart empty. No, not even his rage satisfied, because he still wants to see Robert Willie suffer and he can't reach him anymore. He tries to make a fist and strike out but the air flows through his fingers."

Harvey continued to attend every execution in Louisiana, until his own death from cancer.

The very first person Sister Prejean had contact with on death row was Pat Sonnier, who with his younger brother had abducted a teenage couple, David LeBlanc and Loretta Bourque, raped the girl and then killed them both. It was vicious and brutal. Sister Prejean became Sonnier's spiritual adviser and, as in the Willie case, she came to know the victims' families, the LeBlancs and the Bourques.

Sister Prejean ends *Dead Man Walking* telling about Lloyd LeBlanc, who had lost his young son by Sonnier's act. She writes:

"Lloyd LeBlanc has told me that he would have been content with imprisonment for Patrick Sonnier. He went to the execution, he says not for revenge, but hoping for an apology. Patrick Sonnier had not disappointed him. Before sitting in the electric chair he had said, 'Mr. LeBlanc. I want to ask your forgiveness for what me and Eddie done,' and Lloyd LeBlanc had nodded his head, signaling a forgiveness he had already given ... But (LeBlanc) acknowledges that it's a struggle to overcome the feelings of bitterness and revenge that well up, especially as he remembers David's birthday year by year and loses him all over again; David at 20, David at 25, David getting married, David standing at the back door with his little ones clustered around his knees, grown up David, a man like himself whom he will never know. Forgiveness is never going to be easy. Each day it must be prayed for and struggled for and won."

I cited earlier victims' families seeking the execution of the murderer, as reported in an extensive article in *U.S. News & World Report*. The reporters who gathered the material (Shannon Brownlee, Dan McGraw, and Jason Vest) also reported a number of instances in which victims' families did not seek execution, not finding it helpful in resolving their grief.

William Bonin, also known as "The Freeway Killer," abducted and killed Sandra Miller's 15 year-old son, Rusty. "The rage is unbelievable," Miller said. She nursed that rage for years until Bonin was executed. But Bonin's death brought Sandra none of the relief she had hoped for. It wasn't until she began to learn about the killer's own life, his brutal childhood, that she found some compassion and became able to grieve for her son and to heal.

Some of the victims of the Oklahoma City bombing did not seek the execution of Timothy McVeigh. Marsha Knight, who lost her daughter in the bombing, said she did not support executing him. "If it brought my daughter back, that would be one thing, but it's not going to."

"More often than not, families of murder victims do not experience the relief they expected to feel at the execution," said Lula Redmond, a Florida therapist who works with murder victims' families and is interviewed in the article. "Taking a life doesn't fill that void, but it's generally not until after the execution that the families realize this. Not too many people will honestly say publicly that it didn't do much, though, because they've spent most of their lives trying to get someone to the death chamber."

Grief counselors suspect that some people focus on their hatred of the killer to keep the more painful feelings of sorrow at bay, according to the reporters. Since an appeals process can take years, survivors who nurse their rage may go more then a decade without really grieving.

Prosecutors often stoke a family's rage by telling them that only the death penalty can assuage their sorrow. "When you have lost a child, you go into a state of insanity, and you think whatever they want you to think," says Aba Gayle, 64, of Santa Rosa, California, whose 19 year-old daughter was murdered in 1980. "They told me, 'We are going to catch this man. We are going to convict him, and when we have an execution, you will be healed.' The DA told me this, and the sheriff's department, also the media. And I believed them." Gayle now regrets that and is fighting to keep her daughter's killer from being executed.

A major problem for homicide victim's families can be the criminal justice system itself. The procedures are generally unknown, not easy to understand, and the police and the prosecutors—through overwork, neglect, or uncaring—can be part of the problem rather then the solution.

The reporters state: "The fury often is exacerbated by treatment of the families by the criminal justice system. Sheriff's offices inform them of the death with callous indifference to the shocking nature of the news. Family members regularly travel for hours to attend court only to discover the hearing had been postponed and they weren't notified. Andy Serpico was appalled when, after the 1979 rape and murder of his wife Bonnie, the judge at assailant James Free's trial forced Serpico and his daughter to sit in the back row of the courtroom, while Free's weeping mother was allowed to sit next to the jury."

This discussion of victim's rights and needs has to this point been taken from material dealing with cases in Texas, Louisiana, Oklahoma, and California. Now we need to look at the situation here in Kentucky. In the past 35 years we have had only one execution, and that was of Harold McQueen in July 1997. But during that period we have had our share of violent homicides. As I write this Kentucky has 36 convicted men awaiting execution on death row, and victims' families are struggling to cope with their losses.

Kentucky's experience is similar to those reported from the other states except the Commonwealth has been unique in seeking solutions to the problems victim's families have with the criminal justice system. In the mid-1980s five members of victims' families joined together to do something about the gulf that existed between them and the criminal justice system. As a result of their efforts, the active assistance of the Attorney General, and the public support they engendered, the Kentucky Legislature in 1986 passed the "Crime Victim's Bill of Rights."[39] This Act, for the first time, provided a mandate for law enforcement help and information for victims and deceased victims' families, to assist them with their loss and in understanding the criminal justice system.

39 Kentucky Revised Statutes 421.500 - 421.530.

The Act requires that victims' families promptly receive information on available emergency social and medical services, available crime victim's compensation, and community-based treatment programs. It further requires that they be promptly advised of the arrest of the accused, and how the victim's family can be protected, if needed, as potential witnesses at the trial.

The Commonwealth Attorneys are directed to notify victims and their families promptly of the scheduling, and re-scheduling, of hearings and of all judicial proceedings relating to their case, including the charges placed against the defendant, his pleas, his release on bond, the date set for trial, changes in dates or in the custody of the defendant. It also includes the victim's family's right to present an "Impact Statement" detailing the family's loss and grief for the court's consideration on sentencing or at parole hearings.

The Act further provides that the victim's family shall be consulted by the Commonwealth Attorney on the disposition of the case, including a dismissal, or negotiated plea.

These measures are intended to resolve many of the problems that previously confronted victim's families in Kentucky. The evidence has shown that wherever the local authorities pay attention, the measures are successful. Subsequently, in the 1990s the Legislature has authorized each Commonwealth Attorney in Kentucky to employ a victim's advocate to counsel and assist crime victims and help carry out the mandates of the Crime Victim's Bill of Rights.

This crime victim's movement has also resulted in the formation of Kentuckians Voice for Crime Victims (KVCV), an organization with chapters throughout the state, and with more than 1,800 members. The mission of KVCV is to assist crime victims in the judicial system, in working through their grief, and educating the public about the justice system.

The KVCV does not take a position on capital punishment, but its members have the variety of feelings that I have recounted in this discussion, including many who support the death penalty.

There is an additional victim's family group with members in Kentucky and nationwide — Murder Victim's Families for Reconciliation. The members of this group have undergone the trauma of a family member murdered, and look for resolution of their anger and grief through compassion and the abolition of the death penalty.

The best way to tell their story is through the experience of one of its leaders in Kentucky, Maria Hines.

Hines was born and raised in Virginia with a brother, Jerry, eight years her junior. She and her brother were very close, and she, being the older sister, looked after him. Maria became a nun when she was 19; when Jerry grew up, he became a Virginia State Trooper.

In 1967, Hines decided to leave the convent after sixteen years to become a psychologist and work in the mental health field. This she did, and moved to Louisville where she practiced for many years.

On February 20, 1989, her brother Jerry stopped a suspected drunken driver on a Virginia highway and was shot and killed by passenger Dennis Eaton. When Hines was told of her brother's violent death, her initial reaction was disbelief. For almost a year after the funeral, as she described it, "I walked around in a state of numbness."[40]

Eaton had killed three other persons and was attempting to escape, when he was stopped on the highway by Trooper Hines. When he was later tried, he received three life sentences for those murders, and he waived any right of parole. But, for the murder of Trooper Hines, the state sought and obtained the death penalty. Eaton was sentenced to be executed in Virginia.

When Hines learned of this, she was faced directly with the issue of capital punishment. She could not, in dealing with

40. The material on Maria Hines is taken from personal interviews by the author in 1998 and from an article by Frank Green in the *Richmond (Va.) Times-Dispatch*, May 31, 1998.

her own grief for her brother, understand how another killing would help.

In the spring of 1996 she went to see *Dead Man Walking*. "I not only cried," she said, "but I sobbed throughout the execution scene. I hadn't realized the depths of my feelings. I realized I had to do something."

Slowly, painfully, she came out of her silent numbness and attended a meeting of an abolitionist group, the Kentucky Coalition to Abolish the Death Penalty (KCADP). She found others at the meeting who felt as she did, and that helped.

Her involvement with the KCADP gave her the impetus to tell her story in public, explaining why she was opposed to the death penalty, and why another killing only added to her grief. This was particularly difficult for her to do, because her brother's wife and children did not agree with her beliefs.

But for Hines it was important for her recovery that there be no more killings. She continues to this day, in her own soft and reserved way, to speak out against the death penalty.

As she worked through her grief over the loss of her brother, she wondered about the killer, Eaton. She decided to write him on death row in Virginia. In a December 1997 letter, she wrote:

" ... hell has been defined as the absence of love and, likewise, with hatred instead of love in my heart, my life would be a living hell. So forgiving you is not only for you but also for me - and what it would do to my own soul if I refused to forgive."

Eaton apologized to her and to her brother's family for all he had done, and asked their forgiveness. Her efforts to get clemency for Eaton were unsuccessful, and at the end he asked that she be there at his execution, and to pray for him. She was and she did. The night following the execution she attended a memorial service for Eaton and met a representative of his family, and she took that opportunity to tell him personally how sorry she was that there had been another killing. The two of them held each other; forgiveness and reconciliation had come full circle.

Hines said, "I believe that reconciliation is the next step beyond forgiveness, and I feel privileged that I had this opportunity."

Harold McQueen was executed at the Eddyville Penitentiary in Kentucky on July 1, 1997. His spiritual adviser at the execution was Paul Stevens. This is the other story that needs to be told.[41]

Stevens has suffered as the father of a daughter, Cindy, who was brutally raped, stabbed and killed in 1969 while baby sitting for a neighbor of theirs in Evansville, Indiana. The killer was Jack Gatewood, a man with a history of violence and alcoholism. Stevens vowed Gatewood would be executed for the crime.

The loss of Cindy Stevens, who was only 20, was almost more than Paul and his wife could bear. She was a successful, caring daughter, planning a career in public service starting with serving Native Americans in South Dakota.

The couple attended every day of Gatewood's trial, but Paul Stevens did not get his wish. After a long deliberation, the jury gave Gatewood life imprisonment, and later, because of technicalities, that was reduced.

Stevens was outraged, and the pain of his loss deepened. He could not function well at work and gave up his managerial job. He could not live with all the local reminders of his daughter and her life before the killing, so he and his family left Evansville and moved to Dawson Springs, Kentucky.

But nothing really helped. He was consumed by hate. For eight years Paul Stevens struggled. He had always been a devout Roman Catholic and attended mass every Sunday, but

41. Material on Paul Stevens and Harold McQueen is taken from interviews with Stevens and articles by Judy Morris O.P., "Murder Victim's Dad Becomes Death Row Chaplain," *St. Anthony Messenger*, July 1997, and Nikita Stewart, *The Courier-Journal*, June 22, 1997.

he no longer felt he could receive communion. He had too much resentment and hatred in his heart.

The turning point came in 1978 when he was persuaded to go on a retreat with members of his parish. During his meditations on retreat he began to realize the depth of his bitterness, and in time he grew to understand he did not really want the death penalty for his daughter's killer. He learned to pray in a way that eased away his hate. He began to recover.

In 1986, Stevens responded to an invitation to visit the state penitentiary in Eddyville with Catholic chaplain, Father Frank Roof, and there, for the first time, he met inmates on death row. Stevens found the work and the release he needed, not only for himself but for his daughter, Cindy. He became a volunteer Catholic chaplain at Eddyville, where he serves to this day.

Inevitably, he began to forge personal relationships with the prisoners he met and counseled, including a number on death row. They were, he found, human beings, with terribly broken lives, human beings who had done indescribably horrible things.

Stevens saw many of these men struggling to find some meaning, some purpose in their wasted lives, and some way to repent. He witnessed their battles with their own anger and grief, their begging for forgiveness, their searching for a way to comprehend their horrible deeds. He has witnessed eight men converted to Catholicism, and he has served as godfather to several of them.

Stevens also serves victim's family members who seek out his help. He shares with them his own loss and grief, and how he now serves in his daughter's name and stead, shedding his own hatred. In many instances those seeking his help find their own relief.

In his lay ministry at Eddyville, Stevens met McQueen, who was sentenced to be executed for the murder of Becky O'Hearn, a young woman much like Cindy. O'Hearn had just graduated from college and was clerking in a convenient store in Richmond, when McQueen and two others robbed the store. McQueen shot her twice and killed her, while high on drugs and alcohol. Becky O'Hearn's father wanted McQueen executed, just as Paul Stevens had wanted his daughter's killer executed; but in the McQueen case that was the verdict.

Over eleven years in Eddyville, Stevens and McQueen came to know each other well; Stevens became McQueen's counselor and spiritual advisor. McQueen accepted the Christian faith and began a reformation program and to inform other inmates of the deadly effects of drugs and alcohol.

Stevens says of McQueen, "He's not at all what you'd expect him to be. He's kind and gentle, and he is very sorry for what he did, and the suffering he has brought to others."

Stevens' critics point out that the men on death row, including McQueen, act in a repentant way because they have to, and that they might act much differently if released from prison. Stevens responds, "I don't see how killing Harold McQueen will help anyone. He does important work in this prison and it will be a great loss when he is gone."

McQueen used Cindy's rosary in his prayers up until the night of his execution, and then he handed the rosary back to Stevens and went to the electric chair.

These are some of the stories that tell the tragedy of murders in our society, followed by the families' disbelief, anger, and grief. The loss and the feelings that each individual has when a loved one is murdered are terrible. It is not for me, nor for anyone else, to dictate what those feelings should be, or how they should be resolved, or even if they should be resolved. That is the personal right of each individual, which must be respected.

But we must consider and judge the effect of the execution of the killer in assuaging the anger and grief of the victim's family, in helping to bring closure. What does the execution accomplish?

First, it is clear that when one is hurt this badly, one wants to hurt back. If someone were to take (I cannot say the word, "kill") one of my three daughters, I know my initial reaction would be to strike back. I don't know if I could kill the man but I would want to do *something*, anything, to make the hurt go away. To try and reverse everything. To erase the reality of that death.

Now, the question — is it a good and helpful thing for victims' families to have the state commit that killing in the name of the Commonwealth?

We have seen from many examples, and from the advice of psychologists, that the anger and the hate need to be dispelled before the grief can be effectively addressed. It is the anger and hate that call for an execution.

The difficulty lies primarily in two areas. Because of criminal law procedural safeguards, it is almost always five years or more before an execution can take place. The hatred and anger festers for a long time, and then, when the execution does occur, it is never enough. Few find much satisfaction in seeing a man in shackles killed by the state.

The desire for it to happen may be very real, but the event and its aftermath seldom bring relief. I believe this is the reality for the vast majority of victims' families. The abolition of the death penalty is in keeping with that reality.

THE COSTS

In the discussion of violence and capital punishment we are pursuing, the costs in a capital case seem of little moment. We are debating the health of our society, and our ability to respond to violence in an intelligent and humane way; how then can costs be material or important?

The economic issue is raised by supporters of the death penalty. They argue that the alternative to executions—life imprisonment—is costly, and is an unfair burden on taxpayers.

When we investigate the merits of the argument, we find incarceration costs are, in fact, a relatively small item.

119

What our investigation discloses is that the costs of prosecution and defense in a full-blown death penalty case are an astronomical item. We are talking about millions of dollars of costs that are mostly borne by taxpayers, and are both necessary and inevitable.

To understand this fully, we need to return briefly to the history of capital punishment in the United States. We discussed earlier the case of *Furman v. Georgia*, in which the Supreme Court in 1972 found that the way selected individuals were being tried and sentenced to death in the state courts violated the Bill of Rights, to the point of being freakish and arbitrary — a pattern not serving any legitimate purpose.[42]

The court's opinions reiterated the constitutional safeguards that had to be followed to help the state criminal justice systems be more fair and less discriminatory.

The death penalty states (including Kentucky) read the opinions carefully and rewrote their capital punishment statutes to comply. The basic requirements were: (1) separate trials to determine guilt first, and then sentencing, if necessary (2) the establishment of basic standards for the application of the death penalty sentence, and (3) provision for specific state and federal appellate reviews.

Because death is an extraordinary punishment, these were extraordinary measures, attempting to make the death penalty fair and eliminating past discriminations and past mistakes. The Supreme Court, in *Gregg v. Georgia* [43], approved these changes and authorized capital punishment to begin anew.

The defendant is entitled under the Eighth Amendment of our Constitution to the assistance of counsel, who now has these procedural safeguards to make the playing field more even, and whose sworn duty is to try and save his client's life.

A capital punishment case is very different from any

42. *Furman v. Georgia,* 408 U.S. 238, 92 S.Ct. 2726 (1972).
43. 428 U.S. 153, 96 S.Ct. 2909 (1976).

other criminal case, including any other murder case. Research in the courts shows that in all criminal cases, including murder cases, defendants plead guilty 85 to 90 percent of the time, without the necessity of a trial.[44] The prosecutors and the defense both know basically what the proof will be, the likelihood of a guilty or not guilty verdict, and an agreement is usually reached. The defendant, if he is guilty, knows he is going to be punished and he accepts the best deal, if any, his attorney can get. This is how the criminal justice system works, and how it has always worked in this country.

But a death penalty case is different. As the Supreme Court has said on a number of occasions, and we will all agree, "death is different." When the Commonwealth Attorney decides, as authorized under Kentucky statutes, to seek the death penalty against an accused, it is a declaration of all-out war. No matter how fair and conscientious that decision may be, it remains a demand for unconditional surrender. No matter how damaging the proof may be against the defendant, as long as the prosecutor persists in seeking the death penalty, there are no negotiations. There is nothing to negotiate, unless the defendant is suicidal.

The responsibility of the defense counsel is awesome. He or she is not, as in other cases, just worrying about guilt or innocence, or the amount of time or fines the client is facing. The defense counsel, when facing the client and the work to be done in a capital case, is worrying about whether the client will live or die. It becomes his or her responsibility and burden.

Under these circumstances, it is not only all-out war, it is a long, complicated, almost never-ending war. If there were any fact or witness that might turn the tide, if it were your responsibility, wouldn't you move heaven and earth to find it? If there were any legitimate legal defense that might save your client's life, wouldn't you use it? If there were any argument

44. Barry Nakell, "The Cost of the Death Penalty," 14 *Criminal Law Bulletin* 69 (1978), page 71, citing President's Commission on Law Enforcement and Administration of Justice, *Task Force Report: The Courts* 9 (1967).

that might persuade a court to save your client, wouldn't you make it? The responsibility is all yours if you are defense counsel, and there are no ties. It's win or lose, and if you lose, your client dies.

This is the setting when a death penalty case begins and everyone understands it. It is an adversarial system; each side is going to do everything it can, within the rules, to win. And the costs for both sides fall on the taxpayers of the state, and the county in which the case is tried.[45]

I won't try to give examples of all the ways costs are increased for death penalty cases, but I will touch on a few that will show the broad picture.

The accused will most likely be unemployed and penniless, without any home equity or other property to use to get a loan to pay for his defense. He is entitled to counsel, and it will be provided either directly by the Kentucky Department of Public Advocacy (DPA), [46] or by state contract with a private attorney, willing to take the case at a reduced rate of pay. So, in most death penalty cases we taxpayers pay the costs, both for the prosecution and for the defense.

Of course, in any indigent criminal case the accused is entitled to counsel. But in death penalty cases, the American Bar Association Guidelines for the Appointment and Performance of Counsel in Death Penalty cases (1989) and the guidelines of the Kentucky Department of Public Advocacy, require two trial lawyers to be assigned for the accused because of the extensive preparation required. One lawyer simply cannot handle the workload and the responsibility.

Rich people who commit murders (and there are a number of them), hire expert criminal lawyers who organize

45. Alan F. Blakley, "The Cost of Killing Criminals," *Northern Kentucky Law Review*, Vol. 18, No. 1, Fall 1990, hereinafter referred to as Blakley. Blakley states at page 69, "Between 1930-1967, virtually every person executed was poor." The fact that all Kentuckians on death row are poor and can not afford a qualified attorney, is discussed in Chapter 4, "Death Row."
46. See Kentucky Revised Statutes, Chapter 31.

three or four lawyers, paralegals, investigators, and expert witnesses, into a defense team. These people do not get sentenced to death in Kentucky. The rich may be sentenced to serve a lot of time, but they aren't executed. There are no people on death row who were wealthy at the time of their trial for murder.

At the outset, then, we know in death penalty cases the trial lawyers' fees will be at least twice what they would be otherwise. One of the duties of these attorneys is to raise legal and evidentiary issues by pre-trial motions. Studies show that in death penalty cases the pre-trial motions (those that must be prepared, briefed, and argued before the court) will number between 10 and 25—as compared with the usual five to seven—and tend to be considerably more difficult and complex than in non-death penalty cases.[47]

Trial preparations include investigating the facts, looking for and interviewing witnesses, doing background checks on the principals, performing forensic tests, and seeking expert testimony on any number of crucial issues. Expert witnesses are expensive.

Jury selection is much longer and more complex in death penalty cases. Jurors must be able to consider the full range of punishments provided by statute, but individuals who disclose their opposition to the death penalty in principle are not permitted to serve on the jury.

If the first trial results in a conviction, then the law requires a second, separate trial, on the issue of life or death. This second trial requires different preparation on the facts and events of the defendant's life that shed light on why he should receive a penalty less than death.

If the defendant does receive the death penalty, the statutes provide for appellate review in both state and federal courts. This is a lengthy process, and if the attorneys do a thorough job, as they are required to do by their legal ethics, it

47. Blakley, page 68.

is an expensive process.

In the discussion so far, we have considered this from the defendant's position, but when we turn to look at the prosecution, we find the same dramatic increase in work and expenses. The Commonwealth Attorney has made the difficult decision to seek the death penalty, and he or she naturally wants the jury to reach agreement with that decision. The Commonwealth Attorney has his or her own staff of attorneys —some particularly expert in death penalty cases—and the Commonwealth detectives and police to do investigative work. You can be confident a good Commonwealth Attorney will anticipate all the defenses that may be presented, and he or she will see every stone is turned to rebut every argument. While the prosecutor's costs are more difficult to determine than the defense costs, it is reasonable to judge they are as much increased as the defendant's in a death penalty case.

What do these costs turn out to be? Studies have been conducted in a number of states, including Kentucky, and the results are startling.

Professor Alan Blakley conducted the Kentucky study and published his findings in the *Northern Kentucky Law Review*.[48] He followed two specific death penalty cases in Kentucky, and while neither was completed at the time of his report, the costs to date in the first case totaled between $1.2 and $3.1 million dollars. The second cost between $980,000 and $1.9 million. Those are wide variances, but even the minimum amounts are staggering. And both cases still have a long way to go.

In Florida, studies estimate it costs about $3.2 million to process each death penalty case. In 1988, *the Miami Herald* reported that over $57 million had been spent to execute 18 people, which averages over $3 million per case.[49]

48. Alan F. Blakley,"The Cost of Killing Criminals," *Northern Kentucky Law Review*, Vol. 18, No. 1, Fall 1990.
49."The Costs Associated With Capital Cases," a *Report of the Governor's Task Force on the Delivery and Funding of Quality Public Defender Services*, September 1993, page 1.

In Texas, death penalty cases have been estimated at an average cost of $2.3 million, about three times the costs of incarceration at the highest security level for 40 years.[50]

In California, the *Sacramento Bee* reported it cost California at least $15 million per execution. In New Jersey, the Public Advocate estimated it costs approximately $7 million to sentence a person to death.

A comprehensive study of North Carolina's death penalty costs was reported by Duke University in 1993. Its findings: each execution totals $2.2 million over the cost of a non-death penalty murder case with a sentence of imprisonment for life.

It is clear that death penalty cases are very costly for both the prosecution and the defense. A conservative estimate of current 1998 costs in Kentucky, taking into consideration the studies done here and in other jurisdictions, is approximately $2.5 million per death penalty case taken to completion.

In Kentucky, the death penalty has been sought by Commonwealth Attorneys in 165 cases from 1976 (when the death penalty was reinstated) to 1992 (when these statistics were compiled). Final death penalty verdicts were returned in 28 of them.[51] These 165 death penalty cases, costing in today's dollars an average of $2.5 million. This brings the total to $412.5 million, an average of $25.8 million a year. There were an additional 327 cases of serious capital crimes where the death penalty could have been sought, but were settled by plea bargains or lesser sentences. These cases cost less and have not been included in our totals.

As astounding as it may seem, this is actually what is going on. Tax dollars from the state, and the cities and counties where the cases were tried, are paying these costs.

The next question is, How would these costs be af-

50. As reported, *Dallas Morning News*, March 8, 1992.
51. Testimony and exhibits of Kevin McNally, custodian of DPA homicide records, *Commonwealth of Kentucky vs. Randy Haight*, Indictment No. 85-CR-032, TE Vol. 2, pages 193-225; Appendix A-D, Vol. 6, pages 800-848.

fected if we substituted life without possibility of probation or parole for the death penalty?

We now have in Kentucky a new statutory punishment for capital crimes, passed in the 1998 Legislature, of *"imprisonment for life without benefit of probation or parole."*[52] If Commonwealth Attorneys were to seek this lifetime punishment instead of the death penalty, what would happen to the costs of the prosecution and the defense? The convicted murderer would spend the rest of his life in the penitentiary, but the net costs would be reduced very substantially.

There would be no need for two attorneys at trial — one attorney can handle a murder trial without a death penalty issue. There would be no constitutional need for two trials, as in death penalty cases. One trial would suffice. The appeals mandated in death penalty cases would not apply, and while the defendant would have full right to appeal errors, as in any regular criminal trial, there would not necessarily be the multiple appeals always present in death penalty cases.

What, then, would this mean in reduced costs if life without possibility of parole were the supreme penalty, and the death penalty were abolished?

The average age of the men on death row currently is 40, and they generally have an average life expectancy of 70. It costs $18,000 per year to keep an inmate in maximum security in the penitentiary, plus $1,182 allocated for supervision costs.[53] So the total average cost of a life term for those currently on death row would be $575,460 (30 X $19,182).

The studies we have discussed show the estimated average cost of a death penalty case in Kentucky to be $2.5 million and the average cost for trying a life term case at approximately one third that amount, $833,000. This is a savings of $1.7 million against a cost of life internment of $575,500, yield-

52. Kentucky Revised Statute 532.030.
53. Kentucky Department of Corrections, Planning and Evaluation Branch, publication on cost to incarcerate, fiscal year 1997-98.

ing a net saving per case of slightly above $1 million.

With 36 men currently on death row, the savings would amount to over $36 million.

If we abolish the death penalty in Kentucky, in every case in which the defendant is sentenced to life imprisonment without possibility of parole, it will be more than $1 million less expensive to imprison him for life than it would be to execute him under the current system. In those cases where the defendant is acquitted, or receives a lighter sentence, the savings would be proportionally even greater.

At the beginning of this section, we said that the real thrust of our argument had nothing to do with economics or costs, but concern with the health of our society and our ability to respond to violence in an intelligent and humane way. But when we discover what the costs actually are, we recognize that the death penalty imposes an unconscionable financial burden on state and local government.

In Kentucky, public funds are very limited, and here is a savings available to us that will be constructive for our fiscal health, as well as our social well being.

REHABILITATION

"We can live if we can love."
Dr. Karl Menninger

This is not a time when we hear much talk about rehabilitating criminals. Our rhetoric these days concentrates on punishment. We are "tough on crime." I, too, believe in being tough on crime, if that means dealing swiftly but fairly with offenders, looking to the needs of victims, and offering each one of us an opportunity of living as something other than as a criminal.

But to some being tough on crime means, "once a criminal always a criminal; and the thing to do is lock 'em up, and throw away the key;" or execute!

This attitude has not always prevailed. In our earliest days as a state, those who were helping define our mores, and reflecting the sentiments of our first citizens, wrote:

" ...the reformation of offenders (is) an object highly meriting the attention of the laws ..."

And these same men decried capital punishment, "...which exterminate instead of reforming ... (and) which also weaken the state by cutting off so many, who, if reformed, might be restored sound members to society, who, even under a course of labor might be rendered useful to the community, and who would be living and long continued examples, to deter others from committing the like offenses."[54]

Those were our sentiments when we were a state of some 75,000 souls. Perhaps now, with Kentucky's population at more than 3.5 million, we are less troubled "by cutting off so many, who if reformed, might be restored sound members to society ..."

The proponents of the death penalty argue that murderers cannot be rehabilitated, and if they are executed, they are unable to return to society to murder again. That argument, regardless of its merits, lost all significance when the Kentucky Legislature in 1998 passed an Act establishing *imprisonment for life without benefit of probation or parole* as a punishment a jury may assess for a capital crime. This puts an end to it. If a murderer is beyond redemption, he can now be removed from society for the remainder of his life.

If your response is a skeptical, "I don't believe it – they'll get out," experience has shown you to be mistaken. The law specifically forbids probation or parole, and those are the only two avenues for release, other than a Governor's clemency. The Governor has that power now, so that is not a policy change.

54. Acts of 1798, January Session, Ch. IV, Sec. 1. This first statute of criminal justice in Kentucky is discussed, in Chapter II.

The states that have adopted statutes for a sentence of life without benefit of probation or parole have found that the law works as intended. California has had such a statute since 1960, and not a single person so sentenced has been released.[55]

Even though the "return to society" argument for capital punishment has become a non-issue, it is not really fair to leave it at that; assuming that all murderers placed on death row are beyond redemption.

The man the state executed on July 1, 1997, Harold McQueen, is missed at Eddyville penitentiary because he was a major figure the prison administration used to impress young offenders on the perils of using drugs. McQueen, while on death row, learned to express the pain of his own wasted life in a way that other inmates could relate to, and take to heart. One of McQueen's last activities before being executed was the making of a video in which he talks to young people of the horrors of drugs that he knows first-hand. This video is utilized in Catholic youth programs throughout the state, and thousands of copies have been requested and are now in use in other states. McQueen could have continued this work of helping others, if he had lived. This good work did not reverse the crime he committed, but it was a service of value.

Many of the men on death row, with the help of Paul Stevens and others, have found a spiritual base from which they try to atone for the horrors they inflicted, to seek repentance, and find redemption. While they have by their crimes forfeited their right to live in a free society, this does not end their struggle to find some way to atone, to find some meaning in their existence.

There are national and local studies and statistics on the records of murderers who have completed their terms, or been probated and returned to society. Statistically, as a group they are the least likely to commit another crime.

In a national study of 6,835 male prisoners convicted

55. "No Parole Means What it Says," *San Francisco Chronicle*, April 13, 1990 (citing governor's study).

of homicide who were paroled from state institutions, fewer than five percent of them thereafter were convicted of any crime, and less than one half of one percent committed another homicide.[56]

In Kentucky, following the 1972 *Furman* Supreme Court decision holding the death penalty statutes unconstitutional, the 23 men on death row had their sentences commuted to life imprisonment. Subsequently, 17 of them (74 percent) were paroled. Over the remainder of their lifetimes, four of them committed another offense, but none of them committed another homicide. Their rate of recidivism was about the same as the rate for all parolees.[57]

One other aspect of the argument for removal of murderers from society by execution is the not-often discussed fact that we have made mistakes in whom we select, convict and execute for murder. Since 1970, there have been at least 74 individuals nationwide, convicted and sentenced, waiting for execution on death row, who have subsequently been found to be innocent and released.[58] Fortunately for them, they had not been executed. Once executed, there is little interest in anyone trying to prove innocence; but even so, there have been at least twenty-three cases of innocent individuals who have been executed in the United States.[59]

Reading the accounts of those convicted by mistake, we see the same problems of poverty, low intelligence, poor defense lawyers without the resources to find or use the defenses actually available, and a system that is dead set on moving ahead with being tough on crime. We must recognize the pressure we put on the police to "solve" highly publicized

56. T. Sellin, *The Penalty of Death* (Sage Publications, Beverly Hills, Calif.) 1980.
57. Gennaro F. Vito and Deborah G. Wilson, "Back From the Dead: Tracking the Progress of Kentucky's Furman Commuted Death Row Population," *Kentucky Criminal Justice Statistical Analysis Center Research Report* Series, No. 10, 1986.
58. Death Penalty Information Center, 1320 Eighteenth Street, NW, Washington, D.C. 20036 (www.essential.org/dpic/dpic.r07.html).
59. Michael L. Radelet and Hugo Adam Bedau, *In Spite of Innocense,* (Northeastern University Press, 1992).

murder cases. They must find a "guilty" person, and the prosecutor *must* convict. And there is pressure on the prosecutor to seek the death penalty. These are the realities of our current attitude of being tough on crime.

But, in Kentucky, we have an answer. We have, when it is necessary, the penalty of life *without benefit of probation or parole*. This is a safeguard the people have asked for, and the Legislature has provided. When we abolish the death penalty, we will not lose one iota of the security necessary to keep murderers out of society, and from repeating their offense.

And when we abolish the death penalty, we will no longer run the risk of killing the innocent.

CHAPTER IV
KENTUCKY'S DEATH ROW

"It is the deed that teaches, not the name we give it.
Murder and Capital Punishment are not opposites that
cancel one another, but similars that breed their kind."
George Bernard Shaw, *Man and Superman,* 1903

We have recognized in our review of Kentucky's history an evolution away from the settling of conflict by violence. The abolition of the death penalty is our next logical step, removing this vestige of state-sponsored violence.

In this larger picture, it would make little difference how we currently select those being executed, if we are soon to abolish executions. But, inescapably, when we look on death row and observe the inmates, we realize part of the problem is the system by which they have been selected for execution, and this problem cannot be ignored.

There are, at this writing, 36 individuals on Kentucky's death row.[1] They have the following characteristics in common, in addition to being convicted of a vicious, inexcusable crime:

* Every individual convicted was poor.
* Every individual convicted was male.
* Every individual was convicted for killing a white person.

There is no understanding, or excusing, the crimes. While drugs played a major role in heinous conduct in at least sixteen of the cases, that too, is a choice.

The universal poverty on death row may not explain

1. This statistic is from August 1998 records of the Kentucky Department of Public Advocacy.

the crimes that were committed, but there is no escaping the evidence that their poverty does explain, in many instances, why these particular men were chosen to be executed.

In an earlier section, I talked about the criminal justice system, which I believe in many ways functions well in our society. But, in determining death penalty cases, we have seen the criminal justice system as the ultimate of adversarial contests, and the ultimate in expense.

In a death penalty case, winning for the defense is avoiding death; persuading a jury and a judge, after a guilty verdict, to punish with something, anything, less than death.

Death is the dragon, and the best dragon slayer usually wins. With all due respect to Kentucky's prosecutors, the records show the defense dragon slayers win most of the time.

From the time capital punishment was reinstated in 1976 until 1992, when these statistics were compiled, there were 492 cases of capital murder in Kentucky qualified to be tried as death penalty cases. In 165 of these (33 percent), the Commonwealth Attorneys exercised their discretion and sought the death penalty. In 137 of those 165 cases (83 percent), the defense was successful in getting a result of something less than death. In the total 492 cases qualifying for the death penalty, the defense was successful in avoiding death in 464 of them (94.4 percent).[2]

A review of the cases in which death was avoided does not disclose murders less vicious, or victims' families less devastated. What it does disclose is a number of cases in which prosecutors could have sought the death penalty, but exercised their discretion not to; cases in which the defense attorneys persuaded the prosecutors to accept a lesser sentence; or cases in which the defense attorneys persuaded juries and judges not to impose the death penalty.

A sentence of less than death is not, in capital cases, a

2. Testimony and exhibits of Kevin McNally, custodian of DPA homicide records, *Commonwealth of Kentucky vs. Randy Haight*, Indictment No. 85-CR-032, TE Vol. 2, pp. 193-225; Appendix A-D, TE Vol. 6, pp. 800-848.

rare or extremely difficult result to achieve. Historically, juries and judges in Kentucky are reluctant to sentence an individual to death. Passions do run high in many cases, but there are ways to soothe those passions and present some saving grace in an otherwise gruesome situation. It is the job of the defense to find that saving grace and present it in a way that the judge and jury will be satisfied that the right thing is done in sentencing the defendant to a punishment less than death. Prosecutors know this, and where they are faced with able, well-funded, defense counsel, they will often opt for a lesser sentence, rather than risking a loss.

On death row now sit the 36 men for whom that didn't happen, and it is fair to ask why.

When the United States Supreme Court in *Gregg v. Georgia*[3] authorized the resumption of executions under the states' newly reformed statutes, the implicit assumption was that the execution practices previously described by one Justice of the Court as "wanton and freakish"[4] would be reformed. How valid has that assumption proven to be?

Dr. Gary Potter, Professor of Police Studies at Eastern Kentucky University, and author of numerous books and articles on crime, states the question and the results of his studies as follows:

"In its 1972 *Furman v. Georgia* decision, the Supreme Court struck down the death penalty as arbitrary and capricious, with a significant potential for racial discrimination. In the post-*Furman* era states have revised their death penalty statutes in an attempt to reduce arbitrariness by 'bifurcating' juries, specifying aggravating and mitigating factors for jury consideration, and specifying more clearly death penalty offenses. Has any of this reduced the arbitrariness of the death penalty?

"The research literature answers this question with a resounding, NO! In the post-Furman era defendants in capi-

3. 428 U.S.153, 96 S.Ct. 2909 (1976).
4. 409 U.S.15, 92 S.Ct.2726 (1972).

tal cases are charged differently and treated differently for no apparent or logical reason (Berk, et al., 1993; Gross and Mauro, 1989; Paternoster, 1991)[5]. Sometimes, defendants committing similar crimes with similar criminal histories are charged with capital murder, sometimes they are not. Some get the death penalty after conviction, some do not. Even within the confines of the same state, operating under the same criminal code, varying jurisdictions render varying results. The fact is that even under "reformed" capital punishment statutes, the death penalty is more like a state lottery than a considered act of justice. As one researcher put it: ' ...being sentenced to death is the result of a process that may be no more rational than being struck by lightning.'"(Paternoster, 1991:183).[6]

The inequitable selection process of those to be executed has become so apparent that the American Bar Association House of Delegates, representing 340,000 members, at its annual convention on Feb. 3, 1997, adopted Resolution No. 107, on the death penalty. This resolution was proposed by three separate Committees of the ABA, and the Massachusetts and New York State Bar Associations, and was accompanied by a 14-page report in support of the resolution. The adopted resolution calls for a moratorium on all executions in the United States until death penalty cases can be administered more fairly, impartially, in accordance with due process, and minimizing the risks that innocent persons may be executed.

The areas the ABA found of gravest concern were:

1. Competency of counsel
2. Federal and state appellate justices exercising independent judgment on constitutional issues raised.

---

5. R. Berk, R. Weiss and J. Roger, "Chance and the Death Penalty" *Law and Society Review* 27: 89-110; S. Gross and R. Mauro, *Death and Discrimination: Racial Disparities in Capital Sentencing* (Northwestern University Press, Boston, 1989); R. Paternoster, *Capital Punishment in America* (Lexington Books, New York, 1991).
6. R. Paternoster, *Capital Punishment in America* (Lexington Books, New York, 1991).

3. Discrimination in capital sentencing.

4. Execution of the mentally retarded, and persons who were minors at the time of their offense.

Do these problems exist in the Kentucky experience to warrant our concern? Let's look at some of the men currently on death row in Kentucky and see what we find.[7]

Gregory Wilson, a black man, and a co-defendant white woman were charged with murder, kidnapping, rape and robbery in Kenton County. Wilson's co-defendant employed an attorney, but Wilson, who had no funds, was unable to secure counsel. Just a few weeks before his scheduled trial, the judge posted a notice on the courtroom door "desperately" seeking a lawyer to represent Wilson.

Two local attorneys, neither of whom had ever before handled a death penalty case, responded to the plea. The one who became lead attorney, responsible for the handling of the case, was said to be a heavy drinker and had no established office from which to practice. He gave a bar known as "Kelly's Keg" as his business address and telephone number.

The two volunteers made little or no pre-trial investigation or preparation for the trial. No defense witnesses were called for Wilson and no mitigating evidence was presented on his behalf during the penalty phase. The record on appeal shows there was evidence to present, including a statement of the co-defendant white woman admitting that she inflicted the fatal injury. But the jury heard none of this, only the prosecutor's side, and the jury recommended the death penalty. The attorney for Wilson's co-defendant did present evidence in her defense, and the jury recommended a life sentence for her. Wilson was selected to die. His co-defendant got a life sentence.

Roger Epperson was charged with being an accomplice

7. The facts of the cases discussed in this section are obtained from the archives of the Kentucky Department of Public Advocacy.

to murder, robbery, and burglary in Letcher County. Epperson, with little money, got attorney Lester Burns to defend him. During the time his case was being tried, attorney Burns was personally indicted by the grand jury for mail fraud and conspiracy. We have no way of knowing for sure just how disconcerting this was, but the record shows he offered no evidence on behalf of his client at the trial to decide whether or not Epperson should be executed. The jury gave him the death sentence. Burns has subsequently been disbarred.

Gene White was charged, with two other men, with the murder of three elderly people in Powell County. One attorney represented him and a co-defendant. This co-defendant, with the assistance of their joint attorney, agreed to testify for the state and received immunity. White, who had no funds to secure a different attorney, was tried, found guilty, and sentenced to die. The other co-defendant, who got a different attorney and a separate trial, received a sentence of 20 years. White was the only one selected to die.

In addition to poverty, other elements common to many men currently on Kentucky's death row are mental illness and mental retardation. This should come as no surprise when we see the senselessly brutal crimes for which they've been convicted.

The man expected to be executed next on Kentucky's death row is Eugene Gall, Jr. He was born and raised in Hillsboro, Ohio, suffered brain damage as a youth which brought grand mal seizures, and has a record of being sexually abused. At 22, he was declared incompetent to stand trial in Ohio and diagnosed as paranoid schizophrenic. He murdered in Kentucky, and the defense was mental illness, but the jury convicted and he waits for death, untreated.

David Skaggs was born in a mental hospital to a schizophrenic mother and was convicted in Kentucky of two murders, robbery and burglary. On appeal there is competent evidence that he has organic brain damage and a major psychosis, schizotypal personality disorder, and is mentally retarded.

Because of lack of funds, the testimony of mental incompetency offered at the trial was completely inadequate and the jury recommended the death penalty.

Victor Taylor — convicted of kidnapping, murders, robberies, and sodomy — was diagnosed with congenital organic brain dysfunction, complicated by low intelligence. At age 25, he tested at a mental age of 12 1/2.

Each inmate, of course, has a story, and I have sketched only a few to uncover the prevalence and the problems of poverty and mental illness in those we've chosen for execution. These are two of the types of problems that caused the American Bar Association to speak out.

The ABA, in its investigation, also found evidence of racial bias in the selection of death penalty cases. In Kentucky there are 28 white men (78 percent) and eight black men (22 percent) on death row, while the current proportion of blacks in Kentucky's population is 7.1 percent.[8] But perhaps most revealing and disturbing is how the criminal justice system in Kentucky fails in providing all men with their constitutional guarantee of equal protection. Every black man on death row is there for killing a white person; and there is no person, regardless of color, on death row for killing a black person. That fact discloses a lot about how our system is operating, and it is patently unfair.

And, finally, the ABA raised the issue of our executing boys for crimes committed while a minor.

Kevin Stanford was convicted in Jefferson County of murder, robbery, sodomy and theft. There were two other boys accused along with him, Stanford was seventeen and the other boys were seventeen and sixteen. One boy got nine months juvenile detention. The other boy, whose attorney presented evidence of the boy's mental health problems, received a sentence of life in prison. Stanford, who had a substantial defense that was never presented, received a death sentence.

8. Kentucky Department of Public Advocacy, listing of Kentucky Death Row inmates, August 1998.

In each of these cases a major common problem was inadequate counsel and inadequate funds available at the trial level. This has often been the case, even with the large expenditures that we have noted are made in death penalty cases.

The final case I will discuss is that of Randy Haight, who must be the unluckiest man on death row — a dubious distinction, at best.

Haight was charged in Garrard County with murder and robbery, and the death penalty was sought. He pleaded not guilty.

While the case was being prepared for trial, the defense attorney and the Commonwealth Attorney discussed the possibility of a penalty less than death, should the defendant change his plea to guilty. The Commonwealth's problem was that it had no direct evidence of the defendant's guilt, only circumstantial evidence. The defense attorney's problem was a worry about a potential death verdict. Following these discussions, the Commonwealth Attorney offered this deal: if Haight pled guilty, the Commonwealth Attorney would recommend to the judge a sentence less than death.

When this was proposed to Haight he asked, "Suppose the judge doesn't follow the recommendation?"

Haight was advised that it was the judge's stated position that he did follow such recommendations from the Commonwealth Attorney, and that in fact, since capital punishment had been reinstated, no judge had ever ignored such a recommendation. The Commonwealth Attorney also told Haight that the victim's family had been consulted and had no objection to this plea bargain.

But Haight, under the circumstances was a cautious man. He asked if, once made, he could withdraw a guilty plea if the judge did the unexpected. This, of course, would be up to the judge. The Commonwealth Attorney approached the judge, outlined the reasons for a plea bargain, told him what his recommendation for a sentence would be, and asked if the guilty plea could be withdrawn if, for any reason, he did not accept the Commonwealth's recommendation. The Commonwealth Attorney understood the judge's answer to be, "Yes," and Haight was so advised.

With assurances from the Commonwealth Attorney and on the advice of his own attorney, Haight changed his plea to guilty, to avoid the risk of being sentenced to death, but agreeing to a sentence of life in prison.

Haight is now on death row awaiting execution. The judge, it is reported, received letters from the victim's family and friends prior to sentencing, and announced at the hearing he had decided to give Haight the death sentence because of his guilty plea. He denied Haight's motion to withdraw his guilty plea.

The Commonwealth Attorney and defense counsel joined in objecting and argued against the judge's decision, all to no avail. At the conclusion, Haight exclaimed, "I think I was tricked into this, is what I think."[9]

In our review of those on death row, we find the inequitable conditions that brought the ABA to call for a moratorium on executions do exist in Kentucky. These inequities will be resolved only by a permanent moratorium.

When we attain abolition of the death penalty in Kentucky, we will no longer have the stigma of selecting the poor, the ignorant, the mentally ill, the juvenile, the incompetently-defended, and the unlucky, to be executed. We will put these injustices behind us, and concentrate our energies on the lives and the needs of the living.

9. *Haight v. Commonwealth*, Supreme Court of Kentucky, File No. 86-SC-971-MR; TE 302; A 258. Haight obtained a reversal of this conviction on appeal, but was later tried and his luck was no better, as he again was sentenced to death. See *Haight v. Commonwealth*, 760 S.W.2d 84 (Ky. 1988); *Haight v. Williams*, 833 S.W.2d 821 (Ky. 1992); *Haight v. Commonwealth*, 938 S.W.2d 243 (Ky. 1997).

CHAPTER V
THE NEXT STEP

The next step for Kentuckians in reducing violence is the abolition of the death penalty. There are many individuals and organizations working toward that goal and I will take a brief look at what we know of the public's perception of the death penalty today, and the political realities of achieving abolition.

We have seen in the review of Kentucky's history and laws that our path leads, with some curves and detours, quite markedly towards a less violent society. Although instant and graphic TV reporting pushes violent crime in our face constantly, we know in our private lives and by the statistics that violent crime has decreased remarkably in Kentucky in the past 30 years.[1]

A state execution is a very violent act, done in the name of all of us. How do Kentuckians feel about this? We are fortunate in having some answers drawn from a professional poll taken in Kentucky in 1997 under the auspices of two University of Louisville professors from the Departments of Justice Administration and Sociology.[2]

The poll was conducted as a professional statistical sampling of opinion on the death penalty in Kentucky, and the results were presented in a paper given by the authors at a meeting of the Academy of Criminal Justice Sciences. The paper was entitled, "Kentuckians' Changes in Attitudes to-

1. See the section on Deterrence, in Chapter III, for crime statistics.
2. Dr. Gennaro F. Vito, Professor, Justice Administration, and Dr. Thomas J. Keil, Professor, Department of Sociology.

ward Death Penalty."[3]

 The first striking thing about the poll — and this will come as no surprise — is that a lot depends on how the question is asked. This very factor of how the question is asked gives us an insight into the feelings of Kentuckians on this difficult subject. Here is why:

 When the pollsters asked Kentuckians the stark question, without qualification, "Do you favor or oppose[4] the use of the death penalty for persons convicted of murder," the answer was:

Favor death penalty	69.5 %
Oppose death penalty	14.2 %
Not sure	16.3 %[5]

 When, however, the pollsters asked Kentuckians the question, "Do you favor or oppose the use of the death penalty for persons convicted of murder, if life in prison without parole and restitution made to the victim's family is available as a possible alternative sentence," the answer was:

Favor death penalty	38.2 %
Oppose death penalty	38.0 %
Not sure	23.8 %[6]

 The loss of almost half the support for the death penalty, when there was a real alternative, tells us that it is not the violence of the death penalty that our citizens want, but rather

3. An additional author of the paper was Viviana Andreescu. The paper was presented at the Academy's annual meeting in Albuquerque, New Mexico, March 10-14, 1998, and is referenced herein as Vito and Keil.
4. I have shortened the version from, "In general, would you say you are strongly in favor of, somewhat in favor of, somewhat opposed or strongly opposed to the use of the death penalty for persons convicted of murder, or are you not sure?" Vito and Keil, Note 6, page 28.
5. Vito and Keil, page 18.
6. Ibid. page 18-19.

a sure and severe penalty for violent crime and restitution to victims.

The Vito-Keil poll was also designed to provide a profile of both the supporters and those opposed to the death penalty. The results are interesting. The most significant variant they found was sex. In responses to the unqualified question, do you favor or oppose the death penalty, without the alternative of life without benefit of parole being offered, the number of men favoring the death penalty exceeded the number of women by 20 percent, and in opposition to the death penalty, women exceeded men by 44 percent.[7]

A second important factor was race. In the same unqualified question, as above, minorities supported the death penalty by 18 % less than whites, and more than twice as many minorities as whites opposed the death penalty.

In other aspects, the poll found — contrary to what might be expected — that residents of counties in Kentucky with higher death rates tend not to support the death penalty, and persons who have been victims of violent crime tend not to support the death penalty. Democrats are more likely to oppose the death penalty than Republicans.[8]

The composite poll portrait of the most likely death penalty supporters in Kentucky are white males, under age 47, with less than a college education.[9]

The results in the Kentucky poll generally reflect the national polls–69 percent favor the death penalty nationally if no strong alternative is offered. Some individual southern states, however, are more in favor of the death penalty than is Kentucky—Florida results are 84 percent favoring, Georgia 75 percent, and South Carolina 72 percent.[10]

We can surmise from the polling data that abolition of

7. Ibid. page 12.
8. Ibid. page 16.
9. Ibid. Pages 15, 16, 17.
10. From a poll reported in *The Advocate Journal of Criminal Justice Education & Research*, February 1990, page 32.

the death penalty in Kentucky is politically achievable. We now have a statute making life imprisonment without possibility of parole available as punishment for capital crime in Kentucky, and with that alternative the polls show that 76 percent of Kentuckians are split evenly — 38.2 percent still favor the death penalty, 38 percent oppose. The final decision is up to the almost 24 percent who are undecided.

The purpose of this book is to present to Kentuckians the facts of the case for abolition, with the hope that enough open minds will read and consider, and then vote to abolish the death penalty.

CONCLUSION

"I feel morally and intellectually obligated simply to concede that the death penalty experiment has failed."[1]
Justice Harry Blackmun

We have in these pages discussed in detail what our forefathers so aptly termed, "the last melancholy resource" — state executions. There is a melancholy that spreads and envelops the process of capital punishment. The rituals have a fatalistic tinge, as if inevitable.

Of course, it does *not* have to happen. There is every reason now for us to end the melancholia, and move on.

Deterrence

The supporters of capital punishment have told us that we need executions to deter homicides. We need to show potential murderers, they say, that we are tough on crime and that we will use the ultimate penalty if they kill.

An examination of the real world and the actual facts has shown that it does not work that way. We may wish it were so, that dire threats and action would change murderous conduct, but it is a wish based on a myth. It is not so.

The evidence in Kentucky, and in every state in the nation, is that executions do not deter murderers, do not reduce the number of murders, and, in fact, have no discernible effect on criminal conduct, *except to encourage violence.*

The statistics, while showing that state executions do not deter future murders, also show that state executions bring *increased violence* in their aftermath. We are achieving exactly

1. *Collins v. Collins* 114 S.Ct. 1127.1130 (1994)

145

the opposite result from what we wished.

Every jurisdiction worldwide that has abolished the death penalty has benefited by a reduction in violence. That is the answer to the deterrence theory.

Justice for Society

We have also discussed Kentucky's collective needs and expectations. We want to be as safe as possible, and to feel safe from harm. We empathize with those who suffer from violence, and want to help them, and to see their wrong righted. We want to have justice.

Seeing to our actual safety, through effective laws and law enforcement, is a relatively clear and straightforward task. Reaching out to victims of violence and trying to help comes to us most naturally. But what of our "sense of justice" for society; how can we be made to feel whole?

This is the most difficult challenge because, after a murder, neither the victim's family nor society can be made whole. No matter how much we wish it, how much we bemoan the loss, there is no bringing back what has been taken from us. We are all victims, and we have all suffered a loss. The pain of this is so great, it is no wonder we want to strike out and kill in return.

And what we must face is the fact that killing in return does *not* help. One of the most important observations of this book is that killing in return does not help. It makes it worse. It makes it worse, both for society, and for the victims' family. That is the real truth upon which we must act.

Our gut feelings for revenge, for retribution, for giving what was given, are very real, very natural, and very destructive. When we look back at the history of violence in our Commonwealth, we see the path of this destruction. We see our passions exploding violently in response to the wrongs thrust upon us, and those we thrust upon ourselves. But we can also see the evolution of our better judgment, our understanding, and our compassion.

The early Kentuckians began this journey in 1792, deriding executions, "which exterminate instead of reforming," and proceeded to make the wilderness into a home of farms and villages. We became a part of our country's industrial and social revolutions, exploding into the Civil War. It is in this epoch that we discovered a barbarous violence to revenge the wrongs committed against us. And in the Civil War and its aftermath, there was little end to the wrongs to be avenged.

Our violence may have peaked in the Black Patch wars at the beginning of this century. While we have seen peaks and valleys in the century since, it is my thesis that we have learned and we have worked our way, as we enter the 21st century, toward settling those most egregious wrongs against us, not with violence, but peacefully, and in harmony with each of our individual needs for a spiritual, as well as physical reckoning.

We must stand back and say that what is best for society is not killing, but the providing of safety and protection for each of our members. Executions give us neither safety nor protection, only more violence.

We have available the punishment of imprisonment for life without benefit of probation or parole, when that is necessary; and we have innumerable opportunities to help our children in dysfunctional situations find foundations for growing into healthy, emotionally secure individuals, rather than outcasts. Each child born into violence, whom we can show and offer a way of life in which they can live without violence, will be a grown-up who will not likely use our criminal justice system, nor our penitentiary.

We cannot find justice for our society in executions; but we can strive toward justice with fair, appropriate punishments for criminals, and a helping hand to young people who were unlucky in their life's beginnings, and who are looking desperately to find a way to live and survive. In this way we can find a sense of justice, and a sense of wholeness. And we will be a much better community.

Victims' Families

In our section about victims' families we heard a number of voices; some of them demanding death, others offering forgiveness. Through all the messages lies a heavy pall of pain and sorrow.

What can be done to help? I believe that the first thing we must do is to reach out, to make overtures to complete strangers to tell them that we are sorry, and that we care. There is no lonelier person than one who has lost a loved one to violence.

The second step, I believe, is to recognize the magnitude of the loss, and marshal society's resources to apprehend the criminal, and see that he is fairly tried and, if guilty, punished in a legitimately severe fashion. Each of us owes to the other a full recognition of the loss of a loved one. One human being, taken by violence from the smallest most humble home, in the smallest most humble community, is a human being taken from each and every one of us. If that is not so, then we are not a society, but a barren collection of lonely people.

The third step can be taken only by the individuals who directly suffer the loss, and this, by far, is the most difficult. Each one must face the anger and the pain and the grief, and must find ways to lose the anger, dispel the pain, and gradually relieve the grief. Many who travel this tortuous path ultimately get to the very farthest end from where they started, with forgiveness.

These steps are easy to say here, but so difficult to achieve in real life. But there is one truth that must be recognized from this exploration; killing does not help even the most bereaved victim's family member. Seeking the killing may be all consuming, but accomplishing it is not rewarding. Victims' families do say that forgiveness, if it can be found, does bring a peace.

It is peace and justice that we seek, and they will emerge in abolition.

Costs

I write about the economics of capital punishment with great hesitation, because the subject is so far from the things I believe are really important on this issue. Yet, when I examine the costs, I am astounded and embarrassed by the facts. They cry for attention.

Why should we extol a system of capital punishment that has so many safeguards that each case costs a fortune to try, and the results are so discriminatory we only execute the poor, the ignorant, the ill, and the unlucky. It makes absolutely no sense.

Think for a moment what Kentucky could do with the $1 million wasted on every capital punishment case. There are, for instance, in practically every one of our communities, state and local government and non-profit groups, working with children who have problems. These staffs and volunteers provide care, recreation, love and inspiration for these children, that many would not otherwise have in their lives. This is where crime prevention really occurs, and all of these groups are strapped for funds and facilities and are unable to reach a great many who need help.

Think what grants from the state, gleaned from the savings of a million dollars per death penalty case, could do for these community efforts. We would deter more crime per dollar spent than has ever been achieved in Kentucky, and we would all feel very good about spending the money.

There are no longer any valid arguments supporting the death penalty. We suffer it to exist because we are anxious about our own lives in tumultuous times, and we want something to be done about crime. We are told that to be tough on crime, we must execute murderers. What we are being told is wrong!

The only way to be tough on crime, and get results, is to attack the causes of criminal behavior: absence of family, poverty, drugs, child abuse and racism. But reducing these problems takes time, dedication and skill. It calls for wise and thoughtful expenditures of public funds. This is not flashy work, nor is it easily captured in campaign slogans.

None of us looks for difficult solutions. We all want the quick and easy way, and we have been sold on the death penalty as just that. It is time to re-think that "easy, quick solution."

The death penalty, obviously, is not a solution at all; it is part of the problem.

I believe we are ready in Kentucky to re-think the problem of crime, and to concentrate our energies where they can be fruitful. We are ready to abolish a policy we have outgrown, a policy that is harmful. *We are ready to abolish the death penalty.*

We have done violence. We must now close the second grave.

BIBLIOGRAPHY

Archer, Dave and Rosemary Gartner, *Violence and Crime in Cross-National Perspective*, Yale University Press, New Haven, 1984.

Arnow, Harriette Simpson, *Seedtime on the Cumberland*, The University Press of Kentucky, Lexington, 1960.

Arnow, Harriette Simpson, *Flowering of the Cumberland*, The University Press of Kentucky, Lexington, 1963.

Baldwin, Thomas P., Pamphlet, "Bloody Monday Memorial Services," *Kentuckiana Germanic Heritage Society*, Louisville.

Bedau, Hugo Adam, editor, *The Death Penalty in America, Current Controversies*, Oxford University Press, Oxford, 1997.

Bedau, Hugo Adam, *Death is Different*, Northeastern University Press, Boston, 1987.

Berk, R., R. Weiss, and J. Roger, "Chance and the Death Penalty," *Law and Society Review* 27.

Block, Eugene B., *When Men Play God*, Cragmont Publications, San Francisco, 1983.

Black, Charles L., Jr., *Capital Punishment, the Inevitability of Caprice and Mistake*, W.W.Norton & Co., New York, 1981.

Blakey, George T., *Hard Times & New Deal in Kentucky, 1929-1939*, The University Press of Kentucky, Lexington, 1986.

Blakley, Alan F., "The Cost of Killing Criminals," *Northern Kentucky Law Review*, Vol.18, No.1, Fall 1990.

Burns, Walter, *For Capital Punishment*, Basic Books, New York, 1979.

Castel, Albert, *The Presidency of Andrew Johnson*, The Regents Press of Kansas, Lawrence, 1979.

Clark, Thomas D., *A History of Kentucky*, The Jesse Stuart Foundation, Ashland, Ky., 1988.

Cochran, Hamilton, *Noted American Duels*, Chilton Co., Philadelphia, 1963.

Coleman, J. Winston, Jr., *Famous Kentucky Duels*, Henry Clay Press, Lexington, 1969.

Costanzo, Mark, *Just Revenge, Costs and Consequences of the Death Penalty*, St. Martin's Press, New York, 1997.

Cunningham, Bill, *On Bended Knee*, McClanahan Publishing House, Nashville, 1983.

Cunningham, Bill, *Castle*, McClanahan Publishing House, Kuttawa, Ky., 1995.

Draper, Thomas, ed., *Capital Punishment*, The H.W. Wilson Co., New York, 1985.

Ehrlich, I., "The Deterrent Effect of Capital Punishment," *American Economic Review* 65.

Elliott, Ron, *Assassination at the State House*, McClanahan Publishing House, Kuttawa, Ky. 1995.

Fetterman, John, *Stinking Creek*, E.P.Dutton & Co. New York, 1967.

Foner, Philip S., *The Great Labor Uprising of 1877*, Monad Press, New York, 1977.

Ginzburg, Ralph, *100 Years of Lynchings*, Black Classic Press, Baltimore, 1962.

Graham, Hugh and Ted Gurr, editors, *The History of Violence in America*, Bantam Books, New York, 1969.

Grant, Donald L., *The Anti-Lynching Movement: 1883-1932*, R & E Research Associates, San Francisco, 1975.

Green, W.M., *Capital Punishment*, Harper and Row, New York, 1967.

Harrison, Lowell H., *The Anti-Slavery Movement in Kentucky*, The University Press of Kentucky, Lexington, 1978.

Gross, S. and R. Mauro, *Death and Discrimination: Racial Disparities in Capital Sentencing*, Northwestern University Press, Boston, 1989.

Harrell, Kenneth E., ed., *Public Papers of Gov. Edward T. Breathitt 1963-1967*, University Press of Kentucky, Lexington, 1984.

Harrison, Lowell H. and James C. Klotter, *A New History of Kentucky*, The University Press of Kentucky, Lexington, 1997.

Hevener, John W., *Which Side Are You On ?* University of Illinois Press, Urbana, 1978.

House, H. Wayne, "The New Testament and Moral Arguments for Capital Punishment," *Death Penalty in America*, ed. Hugo Adam Bedau, Oxford University Press, New York, 1997.

Jacoby, Susan, *Wild Justice, The Evolution of Revenge*, Harper & Row, New York, 1983.

Jewell, Malcolm E. and Everett W. Cunningham, *Kentucky Politics*, University Press of Kentucky, Lexington, 1968.

Klotter, James C., *Kentucky, Portrait in Paradox 1900-1950*, Kentucky Historical Society, Frankfort, 1996.

Klotter, James C., *William Goebel, Politics of Wrath*, University Press of Kentucky, Lexington, 1977.

Legislative Research Commission, Commonwealth of Kentucky, "Capital Punishment," *Informational Bulletin No. 40*, 1965

Legislative Research Commission, Commonwealth of Kentucky, "Capital Punishment,"
Research Report No. 218, 1985.

Megivern, James J., *The Death Penalty, an Historical and Theological Survey*, Paulist Press, Wahwah, NJ, 1997.

Montell, William L., *Killings, Folk Justice in the Upper South*, The University Press of Kentucky, Lexington, 1986.

Nakell, Barry, "The Cost of the Death Penalty," 14 *Criminal Law Bulletin* 69, 1978.

Paternoster, R., *Capital Punishment in America*, Lexington Books, New York, 1991.

Pearce, John Ed, *Days of Darkness*, The University Press of Kentucky, Lexington, 1994.

Pearce, John Ed, *Divide and Dissent. Kentucky Politics 1930-1963*, The University Press of Kentucky, Lexington, 1987.

Potter, Gary, "Crime Control and the Death Penalty," *The Advocate Journal of Criminal Justice, Education and Research*, Vol. 19, No. 6, November, 1997.

Powers, Caleb, *My Own Story*, The Bobbs-Merrill Co., Indianapolis, 1905.

Prejean, Sr. Helen, *Dead Man Walking*, Vintage Books, New York, 1994.

Radelet, Michael L. and Hugo Adam Bedau, *In Spite of Innocense*, Northeastern University Press, 1992

Reichert, William O., "Capital Punishment Reconsidered," 47 *Kentucky Law Journal*, No.3, Spring,1959.

Ryan, Perry T., *Legal Lynching. The Plight of Sam Jennings*, Alexandria Printing, Lexington, 1989.

Sellin, T., ed., *Capital Punishment*, Harper and Row, New York, 1967.

Sellin, T., *The Penalty of Death*, Sage Publications, Beverly Hills, 1980.

Short, Jim. *Caleb Powers, and the Mountain Army*, Jessica Publishing, Olive Hill, KY, 1997.

Smedes, Lewis B., *Forgive and Forget*, Harper & Row, San Francisco, 1984.

Smedes, Lewis B., *The Art of Forgiving*, Moorings, Nashville, 1996.

Strean, Herbert and Lucy Freeman, *Our Wish to Kill*, Avon Books, New York, 1991.

Tapp, Hambleton and James C. Klotter, *Kentucky: Decades of Discord 1865-1900*, The Kentucky Historical Society, Frankfort, 1977.

Vito, Gennaro F. and Deborah G. Wilson, "Back from the Dead; Tracking the Progress of Kentucky's *Furman* Commuted Death Row Population," *Kentucky Criminal Justice Statistical Analysis Center Research Report Series*, No. 10, 1986.

Vito, Gennaro F., Thomas J. Keil and Viviana Andreescu, "Kentuckians' Changes in Attitudes toward Death Penalty," *Academy of Criminal Justice Sciences*, 1998.

Von Drehle, David, *Among the Lowest of the Dead*, Random House, New York, 1995.

Walzer, Michael, *Just and Unjust Wars*, Basic Books, Inc., New York, 1977.

Whitman, Claudia and Julie Zimmerman, editors, *Frontiers of Justice*, Vol I, *The Death Penalty*, Biddle Publishing Co., Brunswick, ME, 1997.

Wilson, Samuel M., *History of Kentucky*, Vol II, S.J.Clarke Publishing Co., Chicago, 1928.

Wright, George C., *Racial Violence in Kentucky, 1865-1940*, Louisiana State University Press, Baton Rouge, 1990.

Yoder, John Howard, "Noah's Covenant, the New Testament, and Christian Social Order," *Death Penalty in America*, ed. Hugo Adam Bedau, Oxford University Press, New York, 1997.

INDEX

ABOUT THE AUTHOR

Carl Wedekind is a native Kentuckian who practiced law in Louisville for many years and was President and CEO of the Kentucky Medical Insurance Co. He is active in a number of civic organizations in conservation, civil liberties, and the arts, and currently serves on the national board of the American Civil Liberties Union. He is director of the Abolition 2000 campaign for the Kentucky Coalition to Abolish the Death Penalty. Mr. Wedekind lives in Louisville with his wife, Stephanie, and has three grown daughters, and three grandchildren.